D1567789

Hitler's
CHANCELLERY

Hitler's
CHANCELLERY

Ronald Pawly

The Crowood Press

First published in 2009 by
The Crowood Press Ltd
Ramsbury, Marlborough
Wiltshire SN8 2HR
www.crowood.com

British Library Cataloguing-in-Publication Data
A catalogue record for this book is available from the British Library.

ISBN 978 1 84797 091 6

Frontispiece: Two sentries from the 'Leibstandarte-SS Adolf Hitler' regiment on duty in front of the main entrance to the *Reichkanzlei*, at Voss-Straße No.4.

Editor: Martin Windrow

Typeset by Servis Filmsetting Ltd, Stockport, Cheshire
Printed and bound in Singapore by Craft Print International Ltd

Contents

Acknowledgements

I would like to take the opportunity to thank the following individuals for giving so freely of their time, energy and resources during the production of this book.

My special thanks go to David Chevalier, for sharing a great portion of his knowledge on this subject; Jan Rose, for his help with the photography; and Martin Windrow, for his scrupulous editing of my complex manuscript.

Institutions:
Mrs Kathi Rumlow, Bildarchiv Deutsches Historisches Museum, Berlin; Mr Johannes Rath, Lobmeyr Lusterabteilung/ Chandelier Department, Vienna; Mrs Anne-Dorte Krause, Picture Archive, Deutsches Historisches Museum, Berlin; Ullstein Bild, Berlin; Das Bundesarchiv, Germany.

Photo credits

Editorial note
Readers should note that in an attempt to lessen the unavoidable confusions, we have used throughout this text the form 'Reich Chancellery' for the human organization – the secretariat of state government; but 'Reich**s** Chancellery' for the building on Voss-Straße that it inhabited. Similarly, while the individual street is given as 'Wilhelmstraße', the slang name for the whole Government District takes the definite article – '**the** Wilhelmstraße'.

Introduction

Berlin, on the evening of 30 January 1933: Adolf Hitler, the newly appointed German *Reichskanzler* (State Chancellor, first minister), stands at the open window of a rather shabby, old-fashioned government building overlooking Wilhelmstraße, watching a torchlight procession of thousands of Nazi Party activists and sympathizers marching through from the Brandenburg Gate towards the Wilhelmplatz, cheering his victory and what they believe is their own. The new Chancellor is animated, fidgeting with delight; in the room behind, someone hears him exclaim, 'No power on Earth will get me out of here alive!'.

Berlin, on the morning of 20 April 1939: a few hundred yards away from the window where he had stood to acknowledge the torchlit parade on his first night of triumph, Adolf Hitler is greeted by his most trusted followers and staff as he prepares to meet the guests who have come to honour him on his 50th birthday – bankers, barons of industry, diplomats, the representatives of the influential military, political and civil organizations in this nation and many others. They will gaze around them in awe at the scale and magnificence of his opulent new palace; it is the first model for a whole spectacular new city – 'Germania' – that is already alive in Hitler's mind as a capital worthy of his Thousand-Year Reich.

To the sound of a military band wafting in from an outer courtyard, he stands in a vast, light room 80 feet long, its pale walls decorated with sumptuous tapestries, under two enormous cutglass chandeliers hanging from the ceiling nearly 40 feet above. Soon he will go out, through pillared halls and corridors gleaming with fine marble and gilt, decorated with banks of cut flowers and green boughs. With his most senior generals and ministers, he will be driven through the sunshine to review a huge military parade –

driven between hysterically excited multitudes, half-deafened by the cheering and the pealing of church bells, through a forest of scarlet, black and white flags bearing the broken cross of his new state – the state that he now rules with absolute, unchallenged power. His guests today include the leaders of some nations that he has already cowed into submission; soon, from the Caesarian splendour of his palace, he will unleash his legions on a whole continent.

Berlin, on the evening of 20 April 1945: highranking Party officials, ministers and generals are gathered once again, to wish their Führer a happy 56th birthday. This year the festivities are taking place in what is known as the Führerbunker, more than 50 feet below the same building from which he watched the torches go by just 12 years before. There are not many guests this year; industrialists and foreign ambassadors are conspicuous by their absence, and there is no band playing – in fact there is no pomp of any kind. Those who have attended do so in fear of their lives, and most of them hardly know what wishes to offer Hitler, here below the streets of the capital. Above them, the last few acres of his Thousand-Year Reich are crumbling under Soviet artillery bombardments, and the birthday guests know that in a matter of days the swarming soldiers of the Red Army will snuff out the last resistance among the ruins.

Some of those who are crowded into these cellars will meet again, but only in the dock at the Nuremberg trials. How could any of them have imagined that within so few years the magnificent palace at the heart of the Nazi empire would have shrunk to this – a rat-run of small, dank, noisy concrete shelters? How could they have envisaged that within another month half-starved, ragged Berliners would be picking through the marble rubble in the hope of finding something useful as they face *Stande Nul* – Year Zero?

1   Wilhelmstraße No.77

After 1815, when the Kingdom of Prussia emerged, at last victorious, from the Napoleonic wars, the restored nation became once again one of the major players on the stage of European politics. Throughout the latter half of the 19th century Prussia grew in importance and extended its influence, and in 1866 a long struggle with Austria for dominance of the German-speaking world ended in victory at Sadowa. As the administrative heart of the German Empire founded by Bismarck in January 1871, Berlin's Wilhelmstraße and the surrounding streets became entrenched as the centre of German public affairs, a status that persisted from the days of the Kingdom, through the First Empire (1871–1918), the Weimar Republic (1919–1933) and finally the Third Reich (1933–1945).[1]

What had originally been a wealthy residential neighbourhood, with a high concentration of palaces belonging to members of the Prussian royal family and aristocracy, developed into a government precinct stretching roughly a mile (1.5km) between the Brandenburg Gate and the Leipziger-Platz. In political circles the expression 'the Wilhelmstraße' had the same resonance as 'Whitehall' or 'the Hill' in London and Washington. At the time when Hitler came to power as Reich Chancellor of Germany the bi-centenary of the Wilhelmstraße was approaching; construction had started in 1734 during the reign of King Friedrich Wilhelm I, and soon more than 30 palaces had transformed it into one of the most beautiful neighbourhoods in Berlin.

One of them, standing at No.77, would play an important role during the years of the Third Reich. This palace, consisting of a central building flanked by two wings around an inner court open on the street side, had been built in 1738–39 by the Counts von der Schulenburg.[2] In 1796 the palace changed hands, becoming the property of the Radziwill family.[3]

On 8 October 1862 the former Prussian ambassador in Paris, Otto von Bismarck, became Minister-President of Prussia. Within four years his successful prosecution of the war against Austria, Bavaria and Denmark would allow this extraordinary statesman (himself Danish-born) to engineer the unification of northern Germany. Prussia's victory greatly multiplied its potential manpower and wealth, and inevitably increased tensions with France, then ruled by the Emperor Napoleon III. The latter's grip on power at home was slipping, his failed overseas adventure in Mexico had been costly and humiliating, and France feared Prussian supremacy in central Europe. Bismarck, whose vision and diplomatic skills far outstripped those of Napoleon, was looking for an excuse that would trigger the eventually unavoidable war with France under circumstances favourable to Prussia.

In 1870 such an excuse was provided by Spain, which offered the German Prince Leopold of Hohenzollern-Sigmaringen the throne that had been vacant since 1868.[4] Worried at the prospect of France being surrounded by Germany in the east and a German ally in the south, Napoleon III blocked the candidacy, and demanded assurances that no member of the House of Hohenzollern would ever sit on the Spanish throne. On 14 July 1870, Bismarck published in Paris the so-called 'Ems telegram', a cynically edited version of a conversation between the French ambassador to Prussia and King Wilhelm.[5] Bismarck knew that if France declared war all the German states would unite under the Prussian flag, and that a combination of French incompetence and his own skill had already stripped France of any possible alliances.

On 19 July, five days after the publication of this provocative document, France – as predicted – declared war amid scenes of huge public excitement. She was regarded as the aggressor by the other major powers, and throughout the German states there was an unprecedented outburst of

The Old Chancellery at Wilhelmstraße No.77. In the centre, on the first floor, were the Congress Hall and Hitler's private apartments and office; he retained these after the building of the New Chancellery, and the Führerbunker *was created under the new reception hall built behind the Old Chancellery. The northern range (right) was known as the 'adjutants' wing'. (© Bundesarchiv: 146-1998-013-20A)*

nationalism and patriotic zeal. The outstanding military system created since 1858 by Generals von Roon and von Moltke crushed the French Army in battle after battle, forcing the French to surrender and Napoleon III to abdicate.[6] With victory assured (though Paris was still holding out under siege, and some French armies were still in the field), Bismarck acted swiftly to secure the unification of Germany; on 18 January 1871, in the occupied Palace of Versailles, King Wilhelm I of Prussia was proclaimed Emperor of Germany, with Bismarck as his chancellor.

In 1875, 80 years after the Radziwill family had acquired their palace in Wilhelmstraße, the German Empire bought it for the sum of 6 million gold marks; the money came from France's war reparations. As soon as the building became the property of the state, renovation works began; these would last for the next three years, at a cost of 950,000 Reichsmarks. The resulting Chancellor's Palace was ready in 1878 to host the Berlin Congress, and would retain its function until the end of World War I.[7] Imperial Chancellors succeeding Otto von Bismarck who resided at Wilhelmstraße No.77 were:

Count Georg Leo Caprivi (1890–93)

Prince Chlodwig Hohenlohe-Schillingsfürst (1894–1900)

Prince Bernhard von Bülow (1900–09)

Theobald von Bethmann-Hollweg (1909–17)
Georg Michaelis (16 July–2 December 1917)
Count Georg Hertling (3 December 1917–
    5 October 1918)
Prince Max von Baden (5 October–9 November
    1918)[8]

Following the Kaiser's abdication on 9 November 1918, Prince Max von Baden resigned in favour of the Social Democratic Party chairman, Friedrich Ebert, who was chancellor at the time of the Armistice on 11 November.[9] Although the new government had intended to support a constitutional monarchy, Philipp Scheidemann – concerned by the threat of a workers' revolution in Berlin – proclaimed a Republic without consulting any of his colleagues.[10]

Ebert became the first President of Germany, and moved into Wilhelmstraße No.73; Scheidemann became Chancellor of Germany from 13 February 1919, although he only served until 20

Friedrich Ebert, first President of Germany, February 1919 – February 1925.
(Libary of Congress)

The Borsig Palace, on the corner of Voss-Straße (left) and Wilhelmstraße (right), photographed in the early 1930s. At far left, just above the lorry, note the pillared entrance to the palace, and at far right part of Edward Siedler's extension wing linking the palace to the Old Chancellery.
(© Bundesarchiv: 183-H0115-0500-001)

June of the same year.[11] During the 14 troubled years prior to Hitler's chancellorship, no fewer than 14 chancellors would move into Wilhelmstraße No.77.[12]

During the Weimar Republic the Reich Chancellor's Palace became not only the office of the chancellor but also the seat of the German government. This resulted in a considerable increase in staff numbers, forcing the government to look for other premises. The Chancellery itself suffered greatly from its frequent changes of tenants; each chancellor tended to make a number of interior alterations without undertaking any general restoration or even much maintenance work. At the same time the steady increase in the number of staff and employees requiring accomodation ate away at the official and private appartments orginally available to the chancellor. From a handful of secretaries and orderlies under von Bismarck, the number had risen to 38 permanent staff even by 1919. In the mid-1920s their number had increased to such an extent that plans (dating back to 1913) to build an extension next door at Wilhelmstraße No.78 had to be dusted off.

The Siedler extension

At Wilhelmstraße No.78, between the Chancellor's Palace and the Borsig Palace on the corner of Wilhelmstraße and Voss-Straße, there was now an empty plot of land.[13] This had once been occupied by the Pless Palace, built in 1875–77. Shortly before the outbreak of World War I the German government had bought the palace to obtain space for an extension to the Reichs Chancellery; plans were approved and the palace was demolished, but the outbreak of war halted all further building projects.

On 28 February 1925 Germany's first president, Friedrich Ebert, died, and was replaced in the Presidential Palace at Wilhelmstraße No.73 by the 78-year-old Field Marshal Paul von Hinden-

18 May 1928: President Paul von Hindenburg, accompanied by Chancellor Wilhelm Marx, lays the foundation stone of the new extension to the Chancellery. (© Bundesarchiv: 146-1998-013-26A)

burg.[14] Enjoying great prestige, this respected father-figure was able to bring some kind of stability to German politics (which also resulted in an even larger number of employees in the Chancellery at No.77). On 9 March 1927 the Chancellery opened an architectural comptition for a new building on the empty plot where the Pless Palace had formerly stood.

The immediate problem for the judges was that the new block of offices would have to be inserted between the 19th century Neo-classical Borsig Palace, and the 18th century Chancellery. In all 128 projects were entered for competition, but none of them was judged worthy of receiving the first prize (worth some 7,000 Reichsmarks). With no first prize, the jury also withheld three 2nd and four 3rd prizes; but one of the 2nd prizes (good for some 5,000RM) went to two architects from Berlin: Eduard Jobst Siedler and Robert Kisch, who were awarded the commission to build the new extension to the Chancellery.[15]

Nearly a year later, on 18 May 1928 – the day that could be considered as the 50th anniversary of the Reichs Chancellery – President von Hindenburg, accompanied by Chancellor Wilhelm Marx, laid the ceremonial foundation stone of the new extension.[16] In his speech Chancellor Marx declared that the new building 'should announce that with unpretentious simplicity, but in fearless confidence, they were engaged in the reconstruction of their great German house, the German State'. The new building would demonstrate the values of the new German government, of Berlin and of the Wilhelmstraße to the world, standing as a symbol for an energetic and dutiful Germany.[17]

The building was in a modernist style, with a simple, plain façade covered with smooth limestone slabs. The horizontal lines of the roof and windows followed those of the Borsig Palace and the Chancellery, creating a visual bridge between the flanking buildings. In height the extension followed the Borsig Palace, but to balance the height difference with the lower roofline of the Chancellery the architects designed a tall, square, tower-like annexe, from which they continued the building at the same height as the Chancellery. The interior consisted of a number of ground-

Siedler's extension to the Old Chancellery. Siedler's design followed the general lines of both it and the Borsig Palace, but he added a tower-like construction to the extension to distract the eye from the difference in height between the two buildings.

floor reception rooms, while the upper floors provided offices and six staff residences. In all, the whole project would cost the state 2.4 million Reichsmarks. The impact of the new extension on the Wilhelmstraße would be immense; this was the first time that a modernist building intruded into an 18th- and 19th-century architectural neighbourhood.

During the 1930s all the major political and Party offices would be concentrated along this axis. Hermann Göring, Heinrich Himmler, Reinhard Heydrich, Albert Speer, Martin Bormann, and Hitler himself had their offices in Wilhelmstraße. Joachim von Ribbentrop's official residence as Foreign Minister was located in the refurbished former Reich President's palace at No.73; the Finance Ministry stood at No.61; Joseph Goebbels' Propaganda Ministry occupied Nos.8–9 further south, and the Agriculture Ministry stood at Wilhelmstraße No.72 (as it still does today). The British Embassy was at Wilhelmstraße No.70.

Furniture being delivered to the Siedler building at Wilhelmstraße No.78. (© Ullstein: 00074829)

2   Hitler in the Wilhelmstraße

In May 1932, after two years in government – and like so many before him – Chancellor Brüning resigned.[18] President von Hindenburg appointed the nobleman Franz von Papen as chancellor; Papen immediately called new elections, and in July 1932 the National Socialist German Workers Party (NSDAP) – the Nazi Party – achieved their biggest success yet, winning 230 seats in the Reichstag (the German parliament).[19]

Hitler's National Socialists had become the largest party, and no stable government could be formed without them. Papen offered Hitler the vice-chancellorship, but the latter rejected this and started parallel negotiations with the Centre Party, which was bent on bringing down Papen. In these negotiations Hitler demanded that he must be chancellor, but President von Hindenburg refused.

After a vote of no confidence in the Papen government the Reichstag was dissolved once again, resulting in new elections in November 1932. The Nazis lost seats but still remained the largest party in the Reichstag. After Papen's failure to secure a majority, and the withdrawal of support by General Kurt von Schleicher and the military, the president dismissed Papen and appointed von

The refurbished Congress Hall in the Old Chancellery, photographed between 1933 and 1939. Compare the furniture and carpet with the photos of the State Cabinet Room in the New Chancellery, pages 79–80. (Library of Congress)

The east face of the Borsig Palace and the Siedler building in 1939, after Albert Speer's alterations. At centre is the double gateway leading into the Ehrenhof; at right, the Führer's balcony for reviewing parades, built in 1935.

Hitler's study in the Old Chancellery, with the Lenbach portrait of Otto von Bismarck.
(Library of Congress)

Schleicher as chancellor.[20] Germany was in violent turmoil between the supporters of the Nazis, Communists and Socialists; against a background of major rioting and political assassinations, in January 1933 General von Schleicher had to admit failure, and asked Hindenburg for emergency government powers.

Meanwhile, Franz von Papen, intent on getting revenge for his dismissal, contacted media mogul Alfred Hugenberg and other leading German businessmen.[21] In the past they had supported the Nazi Party financially as a bulwark against Communism, but they were now becoming alarmed by the breakdown of law and order, and due to heavy campaign expenses the NSDAP was on the brink of bankruptcy. At Papen's instigation, these men now wrote letters to President von Hindenburg urging him to appoint Hitler to form a government. At last, with great reluctance, the old president agreed.

On the morning of 30 January 1933, Hitler was chauffered from the Kaiserhof Hotel on the other side of the Wilhelmplatz, and at Wilhelmstraße No.77 (where the president was temporarily in residence, due to renovation work in the Presidential Palace at No.73) he was duly sworn in as Reichskanzler during a brief and simple ceremony.

Hindenburg's presence in No.77 obliged Hitler to move into the Siedler extension; Secretary of State Planck had to leave his residence there so that the new prime minister could move in on 13 February 1933.[22] From the moment Hitler entered the Chancellery he criticized Siedler for having spoiled the Wilhelmplatz's architecture, and complained that the new extension looked like a cigar box – it was unfit to receive foreign diplomats, and unworthy of the new era that had dawned for Germany. He dismissed the new wing as 'fit only for a soap company', and he declared that he would be the first chancellor to rebuild the Chancellery. One of the tales he invented was that the old building had decayed to such an extent that when Hindenburg received him for his swearing-in ceremony the old soldier had warned Hitler to walk very close to the walls, as the floors in the middle of the rooms were unstable.

Two weeks after Hitler moved into the Chancellery, on 27 February, the Reichstag building was set on fire. This act of arson, probably by a deranged Dutch Communist, gave Hitler the excuse he needed to move immediately to curtail all political and civil liberties. Claiming that the fire was the work of a Communist conspiracy, he ordered the closing all KPD offices, the arrest of its leaders and a ban on its press.[23] On 28 February he presented for President von Hindenburg's signature the so-called Reichstag Fire Decree; in the name of 'the suppression of Communist acts of violence endangering the German State', this suspended most of the civil rights enshrined in the constitution of the Weimar Republic since 1919: liberty of the person, freedom of the press and the right of assembly. The police were empowered to enter any premises and to confiscate documents and property at will. Under the constitution the different regions (Länder) of Germany enjoyed partial rights of self-government; the central government of the Reich would now take over the administration of any region that did not take measures to carry out the government's intentions. To back up this draconian decree, the death penalty was also introduced for a wide range of crimes.

30 January 1933: crowds gather in front of the Old Chancellery at Wilhelmstraße No.77 where Hitler was sworn in as Reichskanzler. *It would take him approximately six months to take complete control of Germany. (© Ulstein: 00070219)*

With the Communists eliminated the government still lacked a parliamentary majority, and – in an atmosphere of public hysteria largely orchestrated by the Nazis – Hitler held new elections on 5 March 1933. This time the NSDAP won 43.9 per cent of the vote, and together with their allies of the Nationalist Party (DNVP) they achieved a parliamentary majority of 51.8 per cent.[24] More drastic measures were immediately put in place. On 20 March the government introduced an Enabling Bill, which passed into law four days later; supposedly a temporary response to emergency conditions, to be in force only until 1 April 1937 or until the 'Communist threat' had been eliminated, this law would in practice provide the foundation for the Nazi dictatorship that lasted for the next 12 years.

The remaining democratic liberties of the citizen were removed, and parliament was neutered; in effect, Hitler could rule by decree, and the rule of law was suspended without appeal. On 22 June the sole opposition party, the SPD, was banned.[25] This was followed by the abolition of the free trade unions, and a ban, from 14 July, on the formation of new political parties.

Henceforth the NSDAP and the State became an indivisible and unchallangeable entity; it had taken the Nazis just six months to take absolute political power.

By this time the helpless President von Hindenburg had returned to his Presidential Palace, and Hitler immediately started planning the renovation of the Chancellery.

Albert Speer

In the autumn of 1933 the architect Paul Troost was commissioned to rebuild and refurbish the Chancellery and the Siedler extension.[26] Troost had gained renown for his design work on the ocean liner *Europa* and the Brown House (Braunes Haus) in Munich.[27] His successor Albert Speer would write – in the sycophantic tones that were compulsory during Hitler's years of power – that fate led Hitler and Troost to meet, and to some extent they became friends: 'What Dietrich Eckart was to the Führer for the exchange of ideas about world politics, Professor Troost soon became for architecture'.[28] The reconstruction of the Brown House in Brienner-

The sculptor Arno Breker and Albert Speer, 1942. (© Ullstein: 00010769)

straße in Munich was their first alliance, and they would meet to discuss drawings in Troost's studio in his small house in Theresienstraße:

> In this same studio, plans were made for a new building code, plans for the Königsplatz in Munich, the House of German Art and many other buildings [ordered by] the Führer. The plans for these important buildings were never viewed by the Führer in his official offices. For years he drove to Troost's studio in his spare time in order to look them over. . . . But the Führer did not occupy himself only with the overall outlines: each single detail, each new material received his seal of approval, and much was improved through his fruitful suggestions. Those hours of joint planning . . . became hours of pure joy and the deepest feelings of happiness for him. . . . Here he had the opportunity, during the few free hours that politics allowed him, to dedicate himself to the art of building . . . many beautiful designs were the results of these get-togethers. The Führer found his architect in Troost . . . [who] understood how to interpret Hitler's intentions into the correct architectural form.

But Troost was based in Munich, and unfamiliar with building companies in Berlin; so to assist him, Hitler assigned a promising young architect who had recently done some fine work, to a tight deadline, for Propaganda Minister Joseph Goebbels.

Albert Speer, born in Mannheim in March 1905, followed in the professional footsteps of his father and grandfather. After starting his studies at the Karlsruhe Institute of Technology, he transferred in 1924 to the more esteemed Technical University in Munich, and the following year to the Technical University in Berlin. There he came under the tutelage of Heinrich Tessenow, and became his assistant in 1927.[29] Persuaded by a number of his students, Speer attended a Nazi Party rally in a Berlin beerhall in December 1930, and Hitler made such an impression on him that he joined the NSDAP. A fellow member and close friend, Karl Hanke, recommended Speer to Goebbels, who commissioned the young architect to renovate the Party's district headquarters in

Berlin.[30] The Propaganda Minister was so pleased with his work that he asked Speer to redevelop his Ministry, the former Reichs Press Office; and Goebbels, in his turn, recommended Speer to Hitler. The simple role of a co-ordinator between Troost in Munich and the Berlin construction companies would not last for long, and in late 1933 Speer was given his first official commission for work in the Reichs Chancellery.

During those heydays of National Socialism, Hitler was disturbed daily in his office overlooking the Wilhelmplatz by crowds of admirers outside, who would shout 'Heil Hitler!' in attempts to lure him to the window. Apart from the lack of peace and quiet, Hitler also complained about the poor state of the interior of his office and its limited size (646 sq/ft, 60sq/m), unbefitting the dignity of the new chancellor. He

Albert Speer's German Pavilion for the Paris International Exposition of 1937.

rounding the site with 130 anti-aircraft search-lights. He designed the Berlin Stadium for the Olympic Games of 1936; and at the Paris International Exposition of 1937 his German Pavilion – located opposite that of the Soviet Union, and designed as if a bastion against the onslaught of Communism – earned Speer (like his Soviet colleague) a gold medal.

In 1936, foreshadowing the new architectural style, Speer wrote in *'Die Bauten des Führers'* a fulsome paean of praise of the alleged genius of his Leader in inspiring 'a clarity and strength that will result in an entirely new style of architecture':[31]

> The Führer, too, [like 18th century princes] is a head of state who builds, but in an entirely different sense. His major buildings that are beginning to appear in many cities are an expression of the essence of the movement. They are intended to endure for millennia, and are part of the movement itself. The Führer created this movement, came to power because of its strength, and even today determines the smallest details of its structure. He does not build in the manner of earlier heads of state, who were prosperous contract-givers or patrons; he must build as a National Socialist. Just as he determines the will and nature of the movement, so also he determines the simplicity and purity of its buildings, their strength of expression, the clarity of the thinking, the quality of the materials, and most importantly, the new inner meaning and content of his buildings. Building is not merely a way of passing time for the Führer, but rather a serious way of giving expression in stone to the will of the National Socialist movement . . . the monuments of National Socialism will tower like the cathedrals of the Middle Ages over healthy workers' apartments and new factories.

There are thousands more words of this abstracted fawning, stressing Hitler's uniquely deep and far-ranging wisdom, and the loss to architecture when he regretfully chose to sacrifice himself to his political destiny – we need not weary the reader further. It is interesting, however, that Speer seemed to be sensitive to

Paul Ludwig Troost. This tall, reserved Westphalian belonged to a school of architects who reacted sharply against the highly ornamental Jugendstil, *advocating a lean, restrained approach almost devoid of ornament. He became one of Hitler's favourite architects, and his death after a severe illness was a painful blow; Hitler remained close to his widow.*
(© Bundesarchiv: 102-15444)

ordered Speer to move the office to the garden side, and there followed a complete transformation of the interior, moving walls and corridors. Hitler, who had previously entertained architectural ambitions himself, felt a kind of kinship for Speer, who subsequently became a friend and a prominent member of Hitler's inner circle. As successor to Troost – who died in 1934 – Speer became Germany's leading architect, and would be entrusted with creating a 'National Socialist architecture' in the Classical style.

Soon further official commissions were coming his way, over a range of design disciplines. It was he who created, for the Party Rallies at Nuremberg, the effect of a 'cathedral of light' by sur-

A more distant view of the altered Siedler extension, looking westwards across the new Wilhelmplatz at the southern end of Wilhelmstraße. (© Bundesarchiv: 146-2006-0097)

criticism of major public works at a time when the German population were badly in need of housing. He claimed that 'the increase in new and remodelled buildings in the Reich' was from 159,121 in 1932 to 319,439: 'These figures show more plainly than words the rise in good housing under the Führer's government. This trend will continue and increase significantly once the projects necessary for our security have been completed – buildings that are necessary and which cannot be postponed'. (In fact, by June 1941 it was calculated that Germany had a housing shortfall of 6 million homes; by the end of 1943 the deficit would rise to 11 million.)

Nothing could stop Speer in his ambition, and soon he would be made responsible for one of the most ambitious grand-scale building projects of modern times. In his book '*Mein Kampf*', Hitler had expressed his sadness that Germany's industrialized cities lacked impressive, dominating public monuments. Citing the Colosseum and the Circus Maximus as testimony to the political might and power of the Roman Empire, he wrote that 'Architecture is not only the spoken word in stone, but also the expression of the faith and conviction of a community, or it signifies the power, greatness and fame of a great man or ruler.' In September 1933 Hitler had complained that Berlin was built in an 'unsystematic' manner, and at the beginning of 1937 he put Speer in charge of plans for reshaping the capital into the city of the future – 'Germania'. (This was just a formality, since Speer had been working on the idea ever since he conceived plans for the Olympic Stadium.)

Speer was appointed Generalbauinspektor für die Reichshauptstadt, with responsibility for all construction work in the capital.[32] He gathered around himself a team of famous architects; one of them, Willi Schelkes, later wrote:

I got Berlin-West, which was to become the University City. We were going to combine the University and the Technical Highschool, which had up to then been separate institutions. It was an

exciting innovation, and this huge academic area would also contain and link all the main city hospitals, to provide a new system of health and social care. Additionally, of course, I was put in charge of landscape design for Berlin and its surroundings. Speer's concept, believe me, was incredibly innovative and socially conscious. I know that nowadays people can only think of and condemn the outsize representational buildings, as does Speer himself. But there was so much more, so much to give us hope.

Speer's intention was to create a central North-South axial highway to join the existing East-West axis at right angles in the centre of Berlin. On the north side of the junction he planned a massive forum covering 3.76 million square feet (350,000sq/m) – large enough to contain one million people – around which monumental buildings would rise: an enormous domed People's Hall, Hitler's Palace, the Chancellery, the High Command of the German Armed Forces, and an Arc of Triumph that would tower nearly 400 feet (120m) into the sky. All were to be placed in a strong axial relationship around the forum,

which would be the centre of this grandiose and intimidating display of power.

FÜHRER UND REICHSKANZLER

In May 1934, Hitler was at last able to move into his renovated Chancellery at Wilhelmstraße No.77. (The flat he had previously occupied in the extension building now underwent a complete facelift, and would become the official residence of the Chief of the Reich Chancellery staff, Hans Heinrich Lammers.)[33]

Having centralized in his own hands total power over the political, legislative and juridical life of Germany, Hitler still had to ensure his control of the armed forces – the last important institution that could still (in theory) act independently of his will. Until this time, protected by the presidency of the former Field Marshal von Hindenburg, the Army had been able to maintain a more or less neutral position, but now the aged president's health was deteriorating rapidly. The Army leadership had no objections to an authoritarian government; but a major bone of contention between the chancellor and the Reichswehr was the NSDAP's 700,000-strong political militia, the Sturmabteilungen or 'Assault Detachments' – the SA, popularly known as the Brownshirts.

In Munich in the early 1920s, Hitler had created its beginnings in a gang of former soldiers and beerhall brawlers to act as 'enforcers', protecting the Party's gatherings from interference by the Communists and carrying out reprisals against them. This unpaid, voluntary organization grew rapidly, and some 6,000 SA men paraded before Hitler in January 1923 when he presented standards to their paramilitary regiments. The movement was banned after Hitler's inept attempt to overthrow the Munich regional government by force in November 1923, but this only encouraged its growth in secret. However, when it was reactivated in February 1925 Hitler strictly forbade the movement to bear arms, and this led to a rift between Hitler and the SA leader Ernst Röhm, who left the country.[34]

In 1930, after Hitler invited Röhm back to lead the SA anew, the movement increased enormously in size, and soon dominated the streets. In the aftermath of the Reichstag fire, Hermann Göring – then commanding the Berlin police – authorized the SA to act as auxiliaries, and at Nuremberg in September 1933 some 10,000 uniformed 'Stormtroopers' paraded on Party Victory Day. Röhm was made a member of Hitler's cabinet; but he was never subservient, and never concealed his ambitions for the SA to rival or even to supplant the Reichswehr, from which he had been dishonourably discharged.[35] This made the SA anathema to the armed forces leadership – as did Röhm's hardly concealed homosexuality, the SA leadership's culture of swinishly heavy public drinking, and the SA's thuggish triumphalism in the streets.

With the achievement and consolidation of political power, Hitler did not need the SA any longer; but to pursue his limitless future ambitions he did need the Reichswehr. Something had to be done to correct this imbalance in order to gain the confidence of the armed forces leadership. As Hindenburg grew ever more frail, the chancellor held clandestine talks with the Army high command. The general staff agreed not to oppose Hitler in his ambition to replace Hindenburg as president, combining in his own single person the offices of head of the government and head of state. The only demand pressed by General Blomberg was the elimination of the SA, and in April 1934 Hitler agreed.[36]

On 30 June 1934, on the pretext of foiling a plot by Röhm to mount a coup, Hitler ordered the state Security Police and Heinrich Himmler's smaller but entirely loyal Party 'Self-Defence Squads' – the black-uniformed Schutzstaffeln or SS – to purge the SA leadership.[37] During what became infamous as 'the Night of the Long Knives', Ernst Röhm and probably a couple of hundred other people were arrested and summarily executed – the true figures are unknown. The victims were not limited to the SA senior staff, and the opportunity was taken to murder a number of other opponents of the regime, such as the former chancellor General Kurt von Schleicher.

On the very day after the Night of the Long Knives, Albert Speer received the assignment to renovate the Borsig Palace, adjoining the Siedler extension on the corner of Wilhelmstraße and Voss-Straße, which the government had bought on 23 March 1934 for 1.25 million Reichsmarks. Hitler wanted to move the senior surviving SA leadership from Munich into this building, so that they would be under his constant supervision.

Speed was important, and workers were asked to put in two shifts, day and night, even on Sundays. As with all official construction work, the Nazi propaganda machine elevated it into a prestige project, to be built in the minimum of time and at low cost. Again, walls and rooms were shifted, even staircases were moved, and the first and second floors were knocked through into the Siedler extension linking the palace with the Chancellery. By the end of October 1934 the renovation and refurbishment of the Borsig Palace was complete, and the SA administration moved into 32 of the rooms. However, 12 more were destined for the Präsidialkanzlei (the functionaries of the President's Chancellery) – because, on 2 August 1934, President von Hindenburg had died.[38]

Hitler knew that he now had nothing to fear from the armed forces. Instead of holding presidential elections, his cabinet simply passed a law that proclaimed him, with effect from 2 August, *Führer und Reichskanzler* of Germany. Adolf Hitler was now Reich Chancellor (prime minister); Führer of the NSDAP (leader of the sole political party); the German head of state, and thus commander-in-chief of the Army. All powers in the nation were now combined in his hands, leaving no opponent any legal possibility of challenging his or the Nazi Party's rule.

On 27 August 1934, the staff of the Reich Chancellery swore a personal oath of loyalty to Hitler as Führer of the German State. They were followed by the staff of the president's office – and, on the initiative of Defence Minister Werner von Blomberg, by all members of the Army. Every officer and man now swore personal loyalty to 'the Führer of the German Reich and People, Adolf Hitler', instead of the former oath to 'the People and the Fatherland'.[39]

In late 1934 there was nothing to stop the most powerful man in Germany from realizing his dreams – including his architectural dreams for a new capital.

The first building projects

In his new functions as head of state, Hitler needed suitable premises in which to receive diplomats and hold state receptions, and his first commission was awarded to Professor Leonhard Gall to build a reception hall large enough to accomodate 200 guests.[40] Construction started in July 1935, in the Chancellery garden adjoining the western side of Wilhelmstraße No.77. The simultaneous construction beneath the new wing of an air raid shelter – the future *Vorbunker* – was not made public. Work was completed in January

1936, just in time for the celebrations connected with the Berlin Olympics of that year. Next to this building, a garage and lodgings for drivers, plus a 660-gallon (3,000-litre) petrol tank were also built in the Chancellery garden.

Speer – who had just transformed the Presidential Palace at Wilhelmstraße No.73 into the official residence for Foreign Minister von Ribbentrop – was then approached by the Führer with another, more modest request. For his public appearances, Hitler wanted to add a balcony to the Siedler building; up until then he had been obliged to watch the mass parades on Wilhelmstraße from his window, and actually had to lean out of it to salute them. He preferred to be seen from all sides; he showed Speer a sketch for a balcony, and asked him to turn it into reality. With some adjustments to the Führer's ideas, Speer placed the balcony in front of Hitler's former office on the first floor.[41]

(Propaganda Minister Goebbels again saw an opportunity to link the construction of the balcony in the public mind with the Nazi Party's rise to power, and even falsified the date of its construction. While the first designs for the balcony are dated May 1933, construction work actually only started in the summer of 1935.[42] Hitler himself gave 1934 as the date of construction; and Speer, in his memoirs, dates the building work to 1933.)

The Wilhelmplatz after its renovation, seen from the south. At centre is Joseph Goebbels' Ministry of Propaganda. At left is the junction of Voss-Straße and Wilhelmstraße, with the Siedler extension showing paler between the Borsig Palace and the Old Chancellery. (© Bundesarchiv: 183-S18094)

Step by step, Hitler's ideas were realized. One of the last construction projects in the Wilhelmstraße was a new layout for the Wilhelmplatz. This was surrounded by a double row of mature trees, with statues of six famous Prussian generals standing at the entrances. Now Hitler wanted the square opened up so that it could be used for mass gatherings, visible from his new balcony.

With the main renovation work to existing structures in Wilhelmstraße now complete, Hitler was ready to order Speer to plan and construct a totally new Reichs Chancellery. Before considering this, we should summarize the government machinery that it was intended to accomodate, and something of the use that Hitler made of the executive organs.

The reader trying to grasp this subject should always bear in mind that there was never any coherent distinction between the structures of Party and government power; individuals were often members of both hierarchies in parallel, and also of the SS. There was a great deal of overlapping and contradiction in their responsibilities, and Hitler ruled by deliberately setting one lieutenant or department against another, so that policy could only be pursued by individuals who gained his ear and were given some vaguely expressed general instruction. Hitler made overall policy verbally, in conversations, speeches or press releases; in management terms, the upper echelons of the Nazi state were hopelessly inefficient, and many policies were only translated into action by the ruthless ambition of individuals. (One constant factor, as the war progressed, was that Himmler's SS empire expanded aggressively onto the turf of many other departments.)

THE ORGANS OF GOVERNMENT

Hitler's new position, combining the offices of President and Chancellor of the Reich, had a profound influence on his relationship with the machinery of national government. As head of state, Hitler had the power to appoint and dismiss ministers – previous presidents had been required to consult the chancellor. In accordance with the law of 16 October 1934, concerning the oath taken by ministers and members of the government (which was incorporated within the law of 26 January 1937 on that to be taken by civil servants), these ministers and functionaries owed Hitler unconditional allegiance. The NSDAP's concept of a 'Party Leader' had been extended to the national government, whose members' only function was now to serve as counsellors, abiding by Hitler's will in all things even against their better judgement. The Cabinet was thus demoted from a decision-making body, with the power to overrule the chancellor under certain circumstances, into little more than a rubber stamp for his decisions.

In organizational terms, Hitler would simultaneously be the head of four organs or 'Chancelleries'. Readers should note that in an attempt to lessen the unavoidable confusion, we have used the forms '*Reich* Chancellery' for the human organization, the government secretariat, but '*Reichs* Chancellery' for the building it inhabited:

- The Führer's Chancellery of the NSDAP, directed by Philipp Bouhler
- The Presidential Chancellery, directed by Otto Meissner
- The Reich Chancellery, directed by Hans Heinrich Lammers
- The NSDAP Party Chancellery, directed by Rudolf Hess (1933–41) and Martin Bormann (1941–45) – both Deputy Führers of the NSDAP.

The Führer's Chancellery

Organized by the NSDAP during the Reichsparteitag of 1934, this fell under the direct command of Adolf Hitler himself. It was the means of immediate contact between the Führer and the Nazi Party regarding all questions submitted for the Führer's personal attention; its functionaries dealt specifically with special requests and appeals directed to the Führer. At first the Chancellery was located on the banks of the River Lützow, but it was later brought over to the New Chancellery at Voss-Straße No.4.

The Chief of the Führer's Chancellery of the NSDAP was Reichsleiter Philipp Bouhler. Born in Munich in September 1899, Bouhler – who was badly wounded during World War I – became second secretary of the NSDAP in autumn 1922, Reichs secretary in 1925, and in 1933 Reichsleiter and member of the Reichstag for Westphalia. The post of head of the Führer's Chancellery was created for him on 17 November 1934 (the full title in German was *Der Chef der Kanzlei des Führers und Vorsitzender der Parteiamtlichen Prüfungskommission zum Schutze des NS-Schrifttums* ('. . . and Chairman of the Official Party Inspection Commission for the Protection of National Socialist Literature' – i.e. chief censor). In 1939 the Führer's Chancellery had 195 staff, whose tasks fell largely in three domains.

The most important was dealing with pleas for clemency. From 1938 onwards the Führer's Chancellery had the right to intervene in appeals from Party members sentenced by the courts, though the aim of taking over this area entirely from the Justice Ministry was never achieved. Bouhler's post was one of the internal communication hubs through which Hitler handled correspondence, including letters from ordinary people containing requests for clemency, material help or job procurement, readmittance to the NSDAP, even asking him to be godfather to children or simply sending him birthday wishes. Bouhler was also responsible for Hitler's private correspondence.

The second main area of activity was the granting of stipends, concessions and grants for scientific research. The third was the restrictive laws governing marriage, and orders for forced sterilization under the law regarding the 'Prohibition of Sickened Offspring'. Bouhler also prepared secret decrees before they were brought to Hitler, and it was in this way that he became responsible for activities involving actually killing people – the development and implementation of the Nazis' early euthanasia programme, by which mentally ill and physically handicapped people were murdered during the so-called *Aktion T4*.

As early as April 1939, Hans Hefelmann was ordered to organize the so-called 'childrens' euthanasia', and at some date around the end of that July plans were made to orchestrate the killing of adult mental patients and the physically disabled. A letter from Hitler, dated 1 September 1939 (but probably written in October), names Philipp Bouhler and Hitler's private doctor Karl Brandt as those responsible for euthanasia. Bouhler handed over most of the control of Aktion T4 to Viktor Brack; various organizations were established as fronts for the Chancellery's involvement, including the Gemeinnützige Krankentrapsnort GmbH (Transport of the Sick for the Common Good Ltd) headed by Reinhold Vorberg. Whenever employees of the Führer's Chancellery were involved with this organization cover names were used; Viktor Brack became Jennerwein, Werner Blankenburg was rechristened Brenner, and Reinhold Vorberg was known as Hintertal.[43]

In 1940 Philipp Bouhler, a weak and indecisive figure, found himself a new goal in colonial governance; he actively pursued the post of Governor of East Africa (a colony that the fortunes of war would, of course, fail to return to German control). From 1942 onwards the Führer's Chancellery saw its influence decrease. Appointment to its staff was demoted to common entry with that of the Reich Chancellery, and the manpower demands of wartime had reduced it to 137 people. It now dealt only with appeals for clemency requiring specific interventions, the more common pleas being handed over to Bormann's Party Chancellery.

The Presidential Chancellery

Under the law of 1 August 1934, the Presidential Chancellery was transformed into the *Präsidialkanzlei des Führers und Reichskanzlers*, whose staff was headed by Dr Hans Meissner.

The Presidential office gradually became less important after the Nazis came to power. Under the Enabling Law of 24 March 1933 legislative power was effectively transferred to the Reich government, even empowering it to alter the constitution. Although this law stated that the powers of the Reich President were to remain undiminished, this was flatly contradicted by another article stating that all laws agreed upon by the

Dr Hans Meissner, head of the
Präsidialkanzlei des Führers und
Reichskanzlers. *(© Bildarchiv Preussischer Kulturbesitz)*

cent vote in favour. Otto Meissner proposed that the Reich Chancellery simply absorb the presidency, simultaneously asking to be relieved from office. He was refused on both counts, since Hitler had not yet decided exactly how long the offices would remain bound together.

The Reich President's Bureau was rechristened Presidential Chancellery, and until 1945 would be responsible for appointing civil servants, considering (non-Party) appeals for clemency, granting titles and orders, and all matters of protocol. The Weimar Constitution had not allowed the use of orders and honours, either domestic or foreign, though in practice this rule was never enforced. (Most Länder would continue to issue the Lifesaving Medal, while the Reich President would bestow the Cross of Honour on foreign guests of state – although the German Red Cross was then a private, not a public organization.) In 1922 the Reich President had created the Eagle Shield of

A senior administrator's office in the New Chancellery.
(© Bundesarchiv: 146-1990-048-28A)

Reich government were from now on to be authorized and decreed by the Reich Chancellor rather than by the Reich President – thus effectively stripping the Reich President of his powers. Under Article 48 II of the WRV, only the Reich government were able to 'take measures to ensure the restoration of public order and safety'.[44]

The law concerning the office of German head of state (actually dated 1 August 1934, 24 hours before the death of President von Hindenburg) amalgamated the offices of Reich President and Chancellor; after Hindenburg's death Hitler no longer used the title Reich President, claiming that the 'greatness of he who has just passed away' ensured that the title could not decently be adopted by anyone else. A referendum on the amalgamation of the two offices of state (a meaningless exercise, since the law had already been passed) was held on 19 August 1934, resulting in an 89.9 per the German Reich for intellectual and artistic merit, as well as the Goethe Medal in the centenary year of the great poet's death. These distinctions did not bring the award of insignia, but were simply 'showcase orders'. During the Nazi regime, and especially during the war years, a plethora of titles and orders were created, all of which (apart from Party and allied distinctions) came under the responsibilities of the Presidential Chancellery. There was a consequent increase in personnel, which in itself may have increased activity, but did nothing for the political importance of the presidency.

The State Secretary of the
Reich Chancellery

The concentration of power in the figure of the Führer and Reich Chancellor significantly increased the duties of the prime minister's office, the Reich Chancellery. Even the most minor laws now originated as decrees by the Führer, bypassing the Reichstag altogether. The enhanced position of the *Chef der Reichskanzlei,* Hans Heinrich Lammers, was made public by the fact that new laws – all legal decrees by the Führer, all laws passed by the Reichstag and all common laws – had to be signed by the Führer but countersigned by the Chief of the Reich Chancellery. (After the establishment of the Ministerial Council for the Defence of the Reich in August 1939, all laws required the additional signature of the Chairman of the Council – Hermann Göring.)

Despite the importance of his office, very little has been written about Hans Heinrich Lammers. When Hitler formed his first cabinet in 1933 he surprised many people by inviting Lammers to join it as a State Secretary. Most of the bureaucrats in the Nazi ministries were existing appointments; Hitler could not run the state without them (and anyway, many of them had assisted his rise to power). Only one State Secretary, the lawyer Roland Freisler, was new, while men such as Meissner, Lammers and others were holdovers from the former regime – Meissner in fact served Ebert, Hindenburg and Hitler with equal neutrality.

Lammers was the archetype of a German bureaucrat – a man of whom few Germans had ever heard, despite the presence of his bold, inch-high signature below the cramped scrawl of the Führer on every decree of the Third Reich. At the Nuremberg trials Lammers claimed in his defence that he had merely acted as a sort of 'notary public' or 'glorified postman'. The prosecution thought otherwise: Lammers had been one of the most powerful men in Nazi Germany. He may have lacked the perverted brilliance of Goebbels, the bravado of Göring, the bold genius of Speer; he was an ordinary, unquestioning bureaucrat, with an ordinary bureaucrat's training, but this did not limit him to an insignificant role.

After losing an eye in World War I as an infantry captain, Lammers became a minor official in the Interior Ministry. Disgusted by the weakness of the Weimar Republic, he joined the NSDAP only in 1932, but then betrayed government information to the Party. A specialist in constitutional law, Lammers was responsible for the legislative maze with which the Nazis surrounded their most lawless acts. It was he who created the notorious People's Courts, 'simplifying' the judicial system by drafting a decree empowering the Justice Minister to 'deviate from any existing law'. In his capacity as State Secretary, Lammers played a crucial role in creating new legislation that established a legal foundation for the Nazi state, including the Nuremberg race laws.

Lammers also acted as a filter through which all kinds of legal and administrative information pertaining to the ministries passed to and from Hitler. As State Secretary, Lammers was present at many important Nazi policy meetings (including those from which Aktion T4 emerged), and he cherished a secret pride in his ability to handle the Führer.

Nothing that happened in Germany was beyond or beneath Lammers' passion for detail. The Nuremberg prosecution produced a letter he had written in 1941 to the Justice Minister: 'The enclosed newspaper clipping about the conviction of the Jew Marcus Luftgas to a prison sentence of two-and-a-half years [for the hoarding of eggs] has been submitted to the Führer. The Führer wishes that Luftgas be sentenced to death. May I ask you urgently to instigate the necessary steps.'

Hunched in the dock at Nuremberg (he suf-

Dr Hans Heinrich Lammers, Chief of the Reichskanzlei. *(© Bildarchiv Preussischer Kulturbesitz)*

fered from arthritis of the spine and hardening of the arteries), Lammers was still the perfect bureaucrat; his only concern was an efficient defence, and he spent his time furiously scribbling notes of rebuttal. Interestingly, however, his black American jailer said: 'He is the nastiest old man I ever did see. He growls like a dog when I come near him.'

The increase in Hitler's ostensible workload (and his actual impatience with the opinions of others) led to the gradual cessation of cabinet meetings; the last one mentioned in the cabinet protocol of the Chancellery was held on 5 February 1938. (According to Reichskabinettrat Willuhn, a few more were held during the war; specifically, a cabinet meeting is said to have taken place the day *after* the declaration of war with Russia.) Even major new laws were discussed and drafted in the offices and corridors of the Chancellery rather than during cabinet meetings.

As a result, the Reich Chancellor could now no longer rely on being informed of developments in various departments by their ministers, but had to depend on information provided by Lammers.

The latter thus took on the task of selecting the precise matters to be placed before Hitler for his possible intervention, and thus created for himself the key position of gatekeeper. Reich ministers did retain the prerogative of requesting personal audiences with the Chancellor, but this seldom happened; consequently Lammers became Hitler's sole advisor in many areas, significantly strengthening the State Secretary's position vis-a-vis the ministers. However, Lammers' position in the Reich Chancellery was mirrored by that of Rudolf Hess and later Martin Bormann as heads of the Party Chancellery.

The Party Chancellery

Once in power, the NSDAP retained a bureaucratic organization and hierarchy which paralleled that of the official German government. The Deputy Führer theoretically wielded power nearly equal to that of Reich Marshal Göring (who maintained his position as Hitler's official No.2 until late in the war). As Deputy Führer, Hess and later Bormann oversaw the official finances of the Führer's office and exercised administrative power in Hitler's name. In order to gain access to Hitler, practically every official in the Reich had to go through either Hess or Bormann. Curiously, the office of Deputy Führer steadily lost power and influence under Hess; but Bormann reversed this trend, and became very active in organizing Hitler's personal calendar and making decisions in his name, continuing to plot for and accumulate power until the very end of the war.[45]

The actual work of running the Leadership Corps of the Nazi Party was carried out by the Chief of the Party Chancellery (Hess, succeeded by Bormann), assisted by the Party Reich Directorate, or Reichsleitung; this was composed of the Reichsleiters, the heads of the functional organs of the Party, as well as the heads of the various main departments and offices which were attached to the Party Reich Directorate. Under the Chief of the Party Chancellery were the 42 Gauleiters, each with territorial jurisdiction over a major administrative region of the Party, a Gau. The Gauleiters were assisted by a Party Gau Directorate or Gauleitung, similar in composition and in function to the Party Reich Directorate. Under the Gauleiters came Kreisleiters, each with territorial jurisdiction over a Kreis, usually consisting of a single county, and equally assisted by a Kreisleitung. The Kreisleiters were the lowest members of the Party hierarchy who were full-time paid employees. Directly under the Kreisleiters came Ortsgruppenleiters, then Zellenleiters and finally Blockleiters – responsible for the inhabitants of a single city block.

The following extracts from the 1942 National Socialist yearbook are instructive, despite the turgid language:

> Chief of the Führer's Chancellery of the NSDAP: Reichsleiter Philipp Bouhler
> The Führer's Chancellery ensures the immediate contact of the Führer with the Party in all questions submitted to the Führer personally. There are hardly any sorrows and troubles which are not submitted to the Führer, in boundless confidence of his help. Dealing with pleas for remission or suspension of sentence has developed into a particularly extensive field of activity.

> Reichsleiter Philipp Bouhler
> Berlin W8, Voss-Straße 4. Telephone number for trunk calls: 12 66 21; for local calls: 12 00 54

> . . . As from 12 May 1941 [i.e. following Hess' flight], the Führer has fully resumed the personal leadership of the Party; the agency dealing with the affairs of the leader of the NSDAP is named Chancellery of the Party; its responsible leader is Reichsleiter Martin Bormann.

> All threads of the Party's work converge in the Chancellery of the Party. Here all internal plans and suggestions concerning the Party, as well as all vital questions concerning the existence of the German Nation and lying within the scope of the Party, are handled for the Führer. From here, directives are given for the whole work of the Party either by the Führer himself or by his order. In this way the unity and fighting power of the NSDAP as bearer of National Socialist ideology is guaranteed.

> In order to secure the unity of the Party and State, the following prerogatives within the State have been given to the leader of the Party Chancellery: By the Führer's decree of 29 May 1941, the leader of the Party Chancellery has the status of a Reich Minister and is a member of the Reich Government and of the Council of Ministers for the Defence of the Reich; he represents the Party to the supreme Reich authorities. All prerogatives due to the Deputy of the Führer in accordance with laws, decrees, ordinances, instructions and other regulations hitherto existing, have been transferred to him. They are:

> 1 Participation in the legislation for the Reich and the Länder, including the preparation of decrees by the Führer.
> 2 Assent by the Chief of the Party Chancellery to propose nominations of officials and labour service leaders.
> 3 Securing the influence of the Party upon the autonomous administration of district administrative bodies.

3   *Die Neue Reichskanzlei*

Chronologically, the stages of Hitler's New Chancellery project can be divided into preliminary discussions (1934), planning (1935), demolition work (1936), and construction work (1937).

In his introduction for the book on the New Reichs Chancellery published in 1939, Hitler explained in his own words why he ordered its construction. The mental shift from the problems of easing Berlin's traffic congestion directly to the annexation of a neighbouring country, between the paragraphs prefixed (1) and (2) – *see* page 33 – is rather striking:

When Bismarck decided to purchase the Reich Chancellor's Palace – at that time the Radziwill Palace – after the re-founding of the Reich, his own offices were still located in the Foreign Office. Perhaps the fact that the Reich Chancellor's Palace was situated near the Ministry of Foreign Affairs may have been the main reason for this particular acquisition. The building, which dates from the first half of the 18th century, had virtually no office accommodation of its own. It was an old residence of the nobility, having well-maintained external façades but with highly subsequent internal renovations. These embellishments were carried further at the end of the 19th century, which gradually disfigured the building with those excessive adornments that enabled sumptuous plastering to hide the lack of genuine materials and correct proportions. Even the hall in which the sessions of the Berlin Congress were first held did not escape this process of 'embellishment'. Ugly wall-brackets and an enormous sheet metal chandelier were at that time indeed regarded as special attractions. Such paintings as the building contained were poor specimens provided on loan from Prussian collections; while the portraits of the individual Reich Chancellors – with the exception of a large picture of Bismarck – had absolutely no artistic merit at all.

The park surrounding the building gradually ran to waste. The reluctance to replace old, dying trees with new ones led increasingly to filling up these weatherworn and eroded trunks, at first with bricks and later with concrete. As this practice had continued over a long period, there was no longer any park remaining, but rather a scene resembling the Houthulst forest after three years of British artillery fire [referring to a pre-World War I forest near Ypres in Flanders].

Although the pre-1918 Reich Chancellors restored the building with varying degrees of taste, it gradually became dilapidated after the 1918 revolution. In 1934, when I decided to occupy the building, the greater part of the framework of the roof was rotten and the floors were completely decayed. For the Congress Hall, in which diplomatic receptions were held, a police order restricted the number present at any one time to a maximum of 60 in view of the danger of collapse. A few months earlier, however, on the occasion of a reception of Reich President von Hindenburg, around 100 guests and servants were gathered in one room, with the result that the floor split revealing joists consisting of nothing more than rotten timber which could be crumbled to dust with one's bare hands.

A rainstorm would let in water, not only from above but from below as well, and more flowed into the ground floor rooms from the Wilhelmstraße. In addition, water began to overflow from all available apertures, including the toilets. Since my predecessors could, for the most part, only count on a period of three, four or five months for their term of office, they did not feel obliged either to clear away the rubbish left by those who had occupied the place before them, or to take steps to see that their successors would find an improved situation. They had no formal obligations towards foreign countries, since the latter in any event paid little attention to them. By 1934, the building had thus fallen into a state of complete disrepair, with ceilings and attics mouldering, wallpaper and floors decaying, and everywhere a scarcely bearable stench of decay.

Meanwhile the newly-constructed office block on the Wilhelmplatz side of the Reichs Chancellery, which from the outside gave the impression of a warehouse or of the city fire brigade building, was from the inside like a TB sanatorium.

In order to be able to use the building at all, I decided in 1934 to give it a general renovation. The first reconstruction was not paid for out of state funds but was covered by me personally. It was based on plans by Professor Troost and had the aim, (1) to move the accommodation and reception rooms, as far as possible, to the ground floor, and (2) to equip the first floor for the practical requirements of the Reich Chancellery.

Until then, my office as Reich Chancellor was located in a room that was convenient for the Wilhelmplatz but which in size and layout was rather like the tasteless room of a salesman of cigarettes and tobacco products in a medium-sized enterprise. The heat made it impossible to work in this room with the windows closed, and if they were open the noise was prohibitive. As the Reich Chancellor's receptions had until that time been held in the Reichs Chancellery, and likewise those of the old Reich President (since he lived there while the Presidential Palace was being reconstructed), the upper rooms were set aside for that purpose. However, this of course meant that they were empty and not put to any practical use during the greater part of the year. This was my reason for moving the reception rooms to the ground floor and converting into offices those looking out onto the garden on the vacated first floor. The Congress Hall, which was not used throughout the year, was assigned for Cabinet meetings. As a suitable room for large diplomatic and State receptions did not exist, I decided to give the architect Professor Gall the task of constructing a large hall suitable for the receptions of 200 persons. In conjunction with the redesigning of the lower rooms which was already in progress,

this went at least part way in meeting modest demands in this connection.

But now the merging of the functions of the Reich President with those of the Reich Chancellor, which had taken place in 1934, necessitated not only new rooms for the Presidential staff and the aides of the Armed Forces but also suitable rooms for State receptions. This necessity led in the first place to the acquisition of the Borsig Palace, this being a building which perhaps did not appeal to us stylistically, but which nevertheless was infinitely better than the miserable internal layout of the 90-year-old Reichs Chancellery. Professor Speer therefore received his first commission for the development of the Reichs Chancellery. Within a short period, and without any changes in the external appearance, the building, which had been constructed by the architect Lucea, was brought into line with the factory-type building already constructed in Wilhelmstraße, and was equipped internally on a lavish scale. Momentarily, at least, accommodation had now been found for the Presidential Chancellery, the Armed Forces Adjutancy and the senior SA leadership. The Party Chancellery, presided over by Party-member Bouhler, also received some rooms. The former office building of the Reichs Chancellery was given a balcony on the Wilhelmplatz, the first decent architectural change. Nevertheless these alterations could of course only provide a temporary solution, since they did not solve the main problem.

Then two events occurred which made me decide in January 1938 to provide a permanent solution. They were the following:

(1) To ease the traffic flow through Berlin from east to west, it had been intended to extend Jägerstraße and to project it through the Ministerial garden and the Tiergarten and thus to create a further link with Tiergartenstraße. I considered that these plans worked out by the existing Berlin Urban Building Directorate were faulty, and commissioned Professor Speer to ensure that the necessary relief for the traffic on Leipzigerstraße and the Unter den Linden would be better solved by a straight line west from the Wilhelmplatz. However, this meant that Voss-Straße would

have to cease to be a bottleneck and become a main thoroughfare. Since for obvious reasons this widening could not be achieved at the expense of losing the Wertheim warehouse, this was better achieved on the other side of the street where the Reichs Chancellery garden was located. The need to demolish the whole of this side and rebuild thus followed as a matter of course.

(2) During December and January 1937–38 I had decided to solve the Austrian question, and thereby to set up a Greater German State. Both for its official duties and for its representative functions necessarily linked to these, the old Reichs Chancellery would now no longer be adequate under any circumstances. On 11 January 1938 I therefore entrusted the General Building Inspector, Professor Speer, with the task of rebuilding the Reichs Chancellery in Voss-Straße, and fixed the completion date for this as 10 January 1939. The building was to be handed over on that day.

Although we had already examined the proposal carefully during many meetings, its actual execution was an enormous problem, as the building work could not start before the houses in Voss-Straße were demolished. The end of March was therefore the earliest time when the actual construction work could begin, leaving a building period of barely nine months. That this deadline was achieved is solely due to the merit of this ingenious architect, to his artistic inclination and his unbelievable organizational talent, as well as the diligence of his work force. With this work the Berlin workers outshone themselves. I do not believe that such an achievement would have been possible anywhere else in the world. Conversely, I need not to add that nothing remained undone in the social welfare sphere for those employed on the building. Nevertheless, the completion of this building, when considering the winter and late frost, is only understandable if – as already pointed out – the exceptional productive capacity of the Berlin worker is taken into account.

When Hitler stated that he commissioned Speer to build the Chancellery in mid-January 1938, he ignored the fact that preliminary planning had begun years earlier. Speer himself claimed in his

Speer amd Hitler in discussion over the plans. Hitler usually gave Speer drawings showing how he envisaged architectural features – such as the balcony for the Siedler extension. Speer was skilful at substituting his own designs but still convincing the Führer that they were based upon his original ideas.
(© Bundesarchiv: 183-2004-0312-500)

autobiography that from the moment he received this assignment in 1938 he needed only a few weeks to draw the first sketches – 'forgetting' that some of the drawings were signed and dated by him as early as 1935, drawings showing the State Apartments in their specific order. He preened himself for needing only six weeks to complete the drawings and a year to clear the site, plan the interior of the building, construct the entire complex and furnish it. The reality was totally different.

Early in 1934 the city council of Berlin wanted to trace a new street running from Wilhelmstraße to Ebertstraße through the ministerial gardens, to create better traffic circulation in the district.[46] Hitler disapproved of the idea since it would interfere with his own projects, and therefore proposed that the city council abandon the idea of a new street and replace it by widening Voss-Straße. This is one of the first signs that, even while renovation work was still going on in the Old Chancellery and Hindenburg was still President of Germany, the Führer foresaw a new seat for the head of state, to be not only a seat of government but also his official residence.

Voss-Straße

In the 18th and 19th centuries Voss-Straße, like Wilhelmstraße, consisted of a number of aristocratic mansions, which later housed government departments.

In 1872 the street was constructed to connect Wilhelmstraße with Königgrätzer Straße; it ran through the former property of Count August H.F. von Voss-Buch (1788–1871). This former commander of the Garde Grenadier Regiment 'Kaiser Alexander von Russland' therefore gave the first part of his name to this street, from 2 May 1874 onwards. Among the most important buildings in the 1930s were:

North side (numbered from east to west):
No.1 – Borsig Palace (on the corner of Wilhelmstraße)

The building site of the New Chancellery during construction – a watercolour by Paul Herrmann.

No.2 – Head office of Mitropa, the catering company that had started business in 1916 with sleeping and dining cars for the German rail system.

No.3 – Bavarian Embassy

Nos.4–5 – Justice Ministry of the German Empire, Weimar Republic and Third Reich

No.6 – Head office of the German Reich Railway Co

No.10 – Württemberg Embassy

No.11 – Nazi Party Berlin offices

No.15 – Delbrück Schickler & Co Bank

No.19 – Saxon Embassy

South side (numbered from west to east):

No.20 – Reich Naval Office

No.22 – Mosse Palace (home of the German Jewish publisher Hans Lachmann-Mosse (1885–1944)

Nos.24–32 – Rear of the Wertheim department store

Nos.33–35 – More offices of the German Reich Railway Co

Apart from these, the Jewish-owned Hertie department store had a back entrance on Voss-Straße; the other buildings were mostly residential properties.

The entire Voss-Straße was placed at Speer's disposal, and from 1935 until the end of 1937 Lammers, in the name of the German State, bought one by one all premises in the street that flanked the Borsig Palace and the Chancellery garden. In all, 13.5 million RM was spent; one of the first buildings bought, on 23 October 1935, was the Mitropa head office at No.2, followed in June 1936 by the Bavarian Embassy at No.3, respectively for 950,000 and 1.5 million Reichsmarks.

Hitler spent much time with Speer, exchanging ideas and redrawing plans. After seeing the plans for the State Apartments with the long Marble Gallery he became so delighted that he told Speer 'On the long walk from the entrance to the reception hall [foreign diplomats] will get a taste of the power and grandeur of the German Reich!'. During the next several months Hitler asked to see the plans again and again, but interfered remarkably little, even though the building was

Hitler, accompanied by Speer, inspecting materials for the New Chancellery. (© Ullstein: 00721208)

designed for him personally; he had such confidence in Speer that he let him work freely.

At first the Mayor of Berlin, Julius Lippert, and the city council had enthusiastically welcomed Hitler's and Speer's plans to transform the city as Capital of the German Reich, but when the impact of these works became clearer to them they started having doubts. Lippert's growing resistance was at first tolerated, but when the transformation of Berlin became a priority he became a burden. With Speer working directly under Hitler's supervision Lippert's cause was futile; he was dismissed in 1940, and Speer's path was cleared.[47]

The Saxon embassy at the corner of Hermann-Göring-Straße (left) and Voss-Straße (right).
(© Ullstein: 00397131)

The same corner after demolition and the construction of the New Chancellery. The Chancellery
staff restaurant was on the ground floor at this corner. (© Bundesarchiv: 146-2005-0073)

Construction work

When Hitler commissioned the New Chancellery he asked Speer to ensure that the building would be ready in 1940. However, on 27 January 1937 he informed his architect that the general structure of the building had to be ready on 1 August 1938, and that it must be finished on 1 January 1939 – thus advancing the entire building programme by a year, so that it would be ready for the 1939 New Year diplomatic reception. In the past Speer had already proved his organizational skills; this new deadline will be his ultimate test.

A total of 7,000 workmen worked on the Chancellery (Nazi propaganda raised this number by another thousand). Of these, 3,000 worked in 12-hour shifts, day and night, seven days a week including public holidays. To motivate the workers Speer, with Hitler's consent, distributed free hot soup for those working in Voss-Straße, while the stonemasons received sausage rolls and beer during the evenings. The architect Carl Piepenburg was responsible for the work on the site.[48] To give a good idea of how the new façade would look and how it would fit in with the Neo-classical Borsig Palace, models in 1:1 scale were erected next to the Borsig Palace and at Teupitzer Straße; other models, in 1:10 scale, were used to show the interiors and the Ehrenhof or 'Court (courtyard) of Honour'.

On 2 August 1938, one day behind schedule, the general structure of the building was completed. In good Nazi propaganda style, 4,500 workers were invited to the Deutschland Halle to celebrate the Richtschmaus with Hitler.[49]

But speed had its costs, and the Voss- and Teupitzer-Straße building sites witnessed an unusually high number of work accidents. In August 1938 a workman of the sanitary installation company Alfred Riefenstahl (father of Leni Riefenstahl, the famous film director) died at the Voss-Straße site. Another dramatic accident happened at the scale model site where two brothers, Eugen and Fritz Seyring, both plasterers, died in a fall from scaffolding. To deal with this high number of casualties medical units specializing in construction work injuries were organized in nearby hospitals.

The building site in Voss-Straße. Walls of tall wooden panels were used to screen the work from passers-by (at right) and from the ministerial and Chancellery garden (at left).
(© Bundesarchiv: 146-191-041-03)

Work continued around the clock, illuminated by hundreds of arclights.
(© Bundesarchiv: 146-1973-062-072)

Never in German history had a construction received so much attention as the New Chancellery. The weekly newsreels – *Die Wöchenschau* – kept the German people informed of progress, and on 22 December 1938 Goebbels organized another show in the Deutschland Halle, where Hitler celebrated Christmas with the 7,000 workmen. Every participant received a signed picture of the Führer and a small parcel containing a food ration. At the same time, hot-air blowers were installed in the New Chancellery to dry it out as fast as possible. With the building so near to being ready for handing over to the state, Hitler himself described it:

The ground plan of the building is determined by its function and the area available, and is clear and bold in its statement. The conception of the entire, immense, lateral expanse of the building along Voss-Straße is outstanding, both from an artistic and a technical point of view. The grouping of the inner rooms running from the Ehren-hof is not only appropriate for their purpose, and satisfying in relation to the practical needs, but is also truly splendid in its effect. The artistic layout of the individual rooms, thanks to the contributions of outstanding interior designers, sculptors, painters, etc is truly exceptional. The output of German craftsmen also finds expression here.

On 2 August 1938, the traditional Richtbaum *was erected on top of the completed central wing of the New Chancellery to mark the 'topping out'. (© Ullstein: 00161638)*

The laying out of the garden has been completed up to the section that still has to be used as a building site. The short construction period made it impossible for the auditorium at the end of the large hall to be fully completed in its final form; this area is therefore only temporary, but nevertheless has been taken to a point where the building can be used. Another two years will be needed before this area is finally completed. The Reichs Chancellery building – which is to be used for another purpose from 1950 onwards – represents

Their work finished, 1,400 construction workers were invited into the Ehrenhof *– the Court of Honour – for a meal prepared by the field kitchens and cooks of the Leibstandarte-SS regiment (© Ullstein: 00247842)*

a supreme achievement, both technically and artistically. It pays tribute to the genius of its designer and master-builder Albert Speer.

The chilling reference to 1950 confirms that Hitler intended to build another and even bigger Chancellery in the 1950s; he thought that by then the building would have become too small, and he would need an even more grandiose replacement to be worthy of his new capital city, Germania. This future building would stand opposite the Reichstag; that which had just been completed would be used by Rudolf Hess as Party headquarters.

Workers admiring the Mosaiksaal, *which would in time assume the functions of a sort of pagan chapel for the Nazi regime. (© Bundesarchiv: 183-E00402)*

Hitler and Speer in the Ehrenhof *during a tour of the New Chancellery. (© Ullstein: 00744968 – W. Frentz)*

Office furniture is delivered at one of the two main entrances in Voss-Straße. (© Ullstein: 00067638)

4   Description of the Exterior

Hitler had asked Speer not to make major changes to the aspect of Wilhelmplatz. The exterior of the Borsig Palace was therefore preserved intact, and was entirely integrated into the design of the New Reichs Chancellery. To an observer standing on the Wilhelmplatz the New Reichs Chancellery was largely hidden; the only significant detail that was visible from the square was the double entrance gateway into the Ehrenhof that Speer had constructed in the extension building. The general conception of Speer's plan was as follows:

The West (left) wing, which began in Hermann-Göring-Straße, mainly contained administrative quarters grouped around a patio.

The Central section or *Mittelbau* was set back from alignment with the frontage of the West and East wings by a distance of 16 metres (52ft 6in) towards the garden. This section included the Führer's Study and the offices for his adjutants, the State Cabinet Room and the Great Reception Hall. South of these the immense Marble Gallery formed a wider reception area. The East (right) wing entrance led from the street to offices and working rooms, and could be considered as ancillary to the large reception salons and the Ehrenhof. Ignoring the Borsig Palace facade, the northern side of Voss-Straße thus presented three sections of approximately equal lengths of between 100m and 120m (328ft to 393ft).

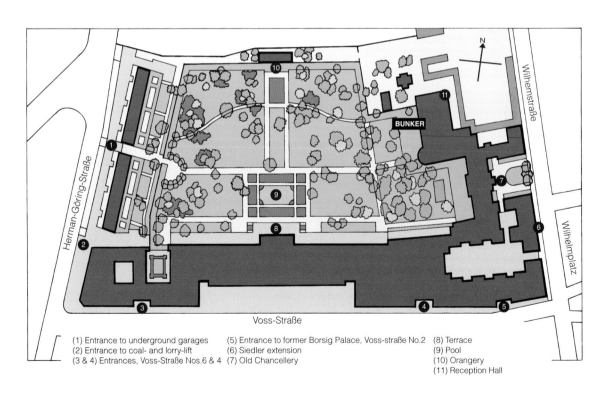

(1) Entrance to underground garages
(2) Entrance to coal- and lorry-lift
(3 & 4) Entrances, Voss-straße Nos.6 & 4
(5) Entrance to former Borsig Palace, Voss-straße No.2
(6) Siedler extension
(7) Old Chancellery
(8) Terrace
(9) Pool
(10) Orangery
(11) Reception Hall

At the Borsig Palace, one portion of which jutted out into Voss-Straße, the height of the storeys in the new frontage conformed to those of the Palace; thus, Speer obtained an optical bridge between the new and old buildings. To achieve this he designed the new façade in such a way that it corresponded with the window size and the layout of the Borsig Palace. The transition to the part which had three floors was effected by the insertion of a large doorway. Another door, the existing entrance to the Borsig Palace, was also inserted between the Palace and the new two-storey façade.

In front of the Central building, five hydraulic doors built into the pavement gave access to an air raid shelter complex underneath the Chancellery.

The two new entrance portals leading from Voss-Straße into the West and East wings were constructed with squared pillars of *muschelkalk* (musselshell limestone) a meter thick and 9m (29ft 6in) high which supported lintels of the same material, surmounted by national emblems (eagles and wreathed swastikas) designed by Professor Kurt Schmid-Ehmen. The wingspan of these eagles measured 7.75m (25ft 5in); the heads of both were turned inwards towards the Mittelbau, in order to accentuate the importance of this central building.

ABOVE: *One of the huge eagles designed by Professor Kurt Schmid-Ehmen to surmount the two main entrances in Voss-Straße; the wingspan was 7.75m (nearly 25 feet 5 inches). The direction of the head shows that this one guarded the left-hand portal, in the West wing – the heads were turned inwards towards the* Mittelbau *or Central wing.*

LEFT: *Sentries from the SA-Standarte 'Feldherrnhalle' regiment – identifiable by their special duty gorget – stand guard at the entrance to the former Borsig Palace at Voss-Straße No.2, where the offices of the SA chief-of-staff were located. After the 'Night of the Long Knives' on 30 June 1934 the chief-of-staff was Viktor Lutze, succeeded after his death in a motor accident in May 1943 by Wilhelm Schepmann. (© Ullstein: 00272324)*

Two angles on the facade of the Mittelbau, *one showing the forward-set balustrade in the foreground.*

This more general view of the Voss-Straße frontage of the New Chancellery shows clearly the Mittelbau *set back from the line of the West and East wings.*

ABOVE: *Detail of the roof eaves, at the eastern corner of the* Mittelbau.

LEFT: *The western – left-hand – portal, at Voss-Straße No.6. The pillars of this monumental entrance were 9m (29ft 5in) tall, dwarfing the two SS sentries in this view.*

BELOW: *The Voss-Straße frontage of the* Mittelbau.

ABOVE: *View westwards along the front of the* Mittelbau, *in the direction of the junction of Voss-Straße with Hermann-Göring-Straße. The balustrade in front of the Mittelbau was aligned with the facades of the outer wings of the building. (© Bundesarchiv: 183-E02115)*

BELOW: *Eastwards view, towards the junction of Voss-Straße with the Wilhelmplatz; note, slanting up between the facade and the balustrade, two of the five hydraulic doors that led to the air raid shelters, here in the open position – see also page 151. (© Ullstein: 00075607)*

The West wing entrance in Voss-Straße, looking to the east. The facade was floodlit in the evenings with searchlights built into the buildings opposite, but in a way that avoided dazzling passers-by.

Flights of steps led up through the portals to doors located in the recessed *muschelkalk* walls beyond. The doors opened into entrance halls, which gave access to the corridors and staircases of the office floors. The design of the doorways embraced the total height of the facade; they were not let into the facade, but were parts of it, giving the maximum effect to their prominent and imposing appearance.

Following Voss-Straße westwards from the Wilhelmplatz, one eventually reached the corner with Hermann-Göring-Straße. Turning right into this street one came to two identical residential-looking white buildings, which served as barracks for the security troops serving at the Chancellery. These stood apart from the Chancellery and had a totally different architecture, being much less ornamental and imposing than the State sections of the complex.

Between the two barrack blocks an inconspicuous steel gate guarded the access road to the two underground garages of the New Chancellery. To

Speer also designed quarters on Hermann-Göring-Straße for the security units that served in and around the Chancellery. In the centre of this photo of the western frontage, an inconspicuous metal gate between the two barrack blocks leads to the Chancellery's underground garages and workshops presided over by the SS officer Erich Kempka, which were situated under the gardens behind these buildings. The lorry entrance to the coal-lift was behind the gate at far right in this photo.

the left was the entrance to the large underground car park where Hitler's chief driver Erich Kempka had his offices, a workshop and quarters for the drivers. In all, Kempka supervised some 60 drivers and about 40 cars. In 1943 an air raid shelter was built into the garage.

Directly opposite the entrance of this underground garage was a service tunnel leading to the West administration block (left wing) and its central courtyard. Lorries had direct access to the delivery zone of the large cafeteria, which was located in the courtyard. But the tunnel was not constructed only for delivery access; the basement under this courtyard also housed the Chancellery's fire brigade, and from the courtyard there was direct access to the gardens behind the guards' barracks in Hermann-Göring-Straße.

Looking at the northern façade of the Chancellery from the garden behind it, one got the impression that it was a totally different building from the one seen from Voss-Straße. The garden was dominated by the Mittelbau, which was 189m

(620ft) long. Access to the garden was via a terrace, 10m longer than the Mittelbau, 9.5m wide and c.3m high from ground level (652ft by 31ft by 9ft 10in high). The flights of steps leading up to the terrace at each end were masked by the integrated plinths of two gigantic bronze horse statues, and were not immediately apparent from across the garden. The horses, for which the originals were sculpted by Professor Thorak, had a strongly modelled nobility that blended well with the classical façade.

This northern façade of the Central block had a facing of *muschelkalk* trim surrounding areas covered with yellow roughcast. The most striking feature of the design of this face was provided by the fluted marble columns in front of the Führer's Study. These stood in four pairs flanked by two single columns, and rose to foliate capitals in the Egyptian style that were partially covered with gilded bronze. The portal itself was picked out in some of the materials that were used for the Führer's Study. Behind these columns, five tall French windows gave access to the terrace from

The central range of the Chancellery seen from the garden, looking to the south-west.

Hitler's study, and also provided the best view of the garden.

To the east of the terrace ran a vaulted colonnade constructed with large blocks of *muschelkalk*. This stood between the garden and the State Dining Room, which could be entered through high, rounded doors. Above the dining room, on the first floor, was the Library overlooking the garden.

To the west of the terrace, a pergola passageway led from the patio behind the West wing (though without access from it), up the west side of the Chancellery garden along the wall separating it from the garden of the guard barracks, then 90° right towards a greenhouse centred at the northern side of the garden. In fact, in design and

The terrace and steps outside Hitler's study – behind the columns – looking to the south-east. This gives little sense of the positively Roman scale; the terrace was 190m (nearly 208 yards) long by 9.5m (more than 10 yards) wide, and stood 3m (nearly 10 feet) high above garden level.

function this was more properly called an orangery, as traditionally found in the grounds of many aristocratic properties. This building, constructed of tufaceous limestone, was located directly opposite the Führer's Study; its front wall consisted of large French doors with narrow glazing bars. Hitler wished to be surrounded by opulence fit for a modest palace, and at his demand two large sculptures were placed to flank the front of the orangery.

Below the terrace was an ornamental pool, also aligned with the orangery.[50]

In the north-eastern corner of the garden Speer built an additional two-storey house for some of the Chancellery staff. Usually known as the Kempka House, after the head of Hitler's motor pool, this stood close to the new reception hall that had been added by Gall behind the Old Chancellery in 1935–36, and adjoined the Foreign Ministry garden to the north.

Detail of the gilt bronze decoration of the column capitals.

The French windows from Hitler's study, here mostly hidden by the marble columns above the terrace.

At each side of the terrace above the masked flights of steps stood a giant bronze horse, by Thorak. This view to the north-west from the eastern end of the terrace also shows, in the middleground, the ornamental pool.

Professor Thorak at work in the studio – this gives a better immediate idea of the scale of the horses guarding the Führer's terrace. (© Bundesarchiv: 183-R65356)

Style of the rear façade of the Mittelbau, *facing on to the garden on both sides of the terrace.*

Looking south from the garden at the colonnade along the rear of the East wing, leading between the terrace (to the right) and the Old Chancellery (to the left). Beyond it lay the State Dining Room, with the Library above it on the first floor.

LEFT: *Interior of the vaulted colonnade, looking west, with the dining room to the left and the garden to the right.*

BELOW: *The greenhouse or orangery at the north side of the garden, centred directly opposite the pool, the terrace and the French windows from Hitler's study. Note the statues at either side of the façade.*

ABOVE AND BELOW: *Exterior and interior of the orangery.*

ABOVE: *Western end of the orangery, with one of the bronze statues. To the left, a pergola or covered passageway follows the garden wall to the west, in the direction of the northern end of the barrack blocks. At the north-west corner this turned 90° south and followed the wall separating the Chancellery and barracks gardens, ending at the patio at the rear of the West wing.*

5 Description – the State Apartments

Speer recollected that Hitler asked him to construct an architectural stage-set of imperial majesty, and to provide large rooms and halls to intimidate lesser potentates. Enjoying an unrestricted and undisclosed budget, Speer produced exactly what Hitler desired.

The main entrance doors on Wilhelmstraße, leading to the Ehrenhof.   ABOVE: *The Mosaic Hall.*

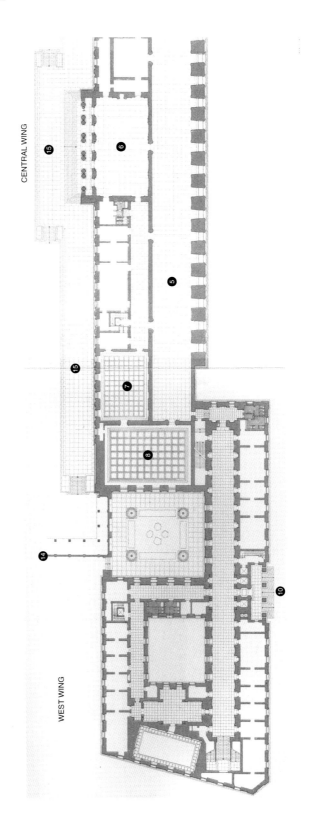

CENTRAL WING

WEST WING

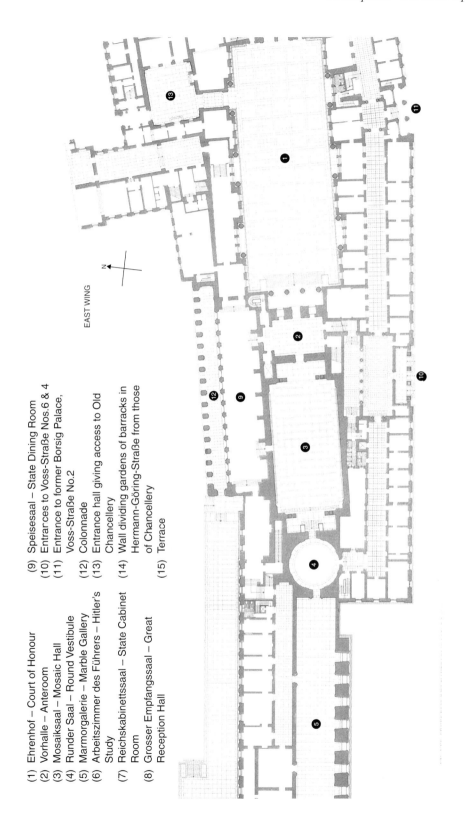

(1) Ehrenhof – Court of Honour
(2) Vorhalle – Anteroom
(3) Mosaiksaal – Mosaic Hall
(4) Runder Saal – Round Vestibule
(5) Marmorgalerie – Marble Gallery
(6) Arbeitszimmer des Führers – Hitler's Study
(7) Reichskabinettssaal – State Cabinet Room
(8) Grosser Empfangssaal – Great Reception Hall

(9) Speisesaal – State Dining Room
(10) Entrances to Voss-Straße Nos.6 & 4
(11) Entrance to former Borsig Palace, Voss-Straße No.2
(12) Colonnade
(13) Entrance hall giving access to Old Chancellery
(14) Wall dividing gardens of barracks in Hermann-Göring-Straße from those of Chancellery
(15) Terrace

EAST WING

On entering the Court of Honour, the visitor confronted at the far end the doors into the Anteroom, flanked by two giant bronze statues by Arno Breker: to the left stood 'Party', to the right 'Armed Forces'. Above the door was another huge bronze eagle designed by Kurt Schmid-Ehmen, this one with half-folded wings.

THE *EHRENHOF* (COURT OF HONOUR)

The Ehrenhof was entered from Wilhemstraße by way of two heavy bronze doors. This courtyard measured 68m in length and 26m wide (223ft by 85ft 4in). Its inner walls were constructed from Jura dolomite. The north and south side walls, pierced by the windows of the surrounding rooms, were each divided into six sections, of which three were recesses flanked by cylindrical columns of the same stone. The fine grey material used and the elegant mouldings gave, in Wilhelm Lotz's words, an impression of 'solemn peace'. From the north side of the Ehrenhof, close to the Wilhelmstraße entrance, a passageway led into an entrance hall and thence towards Hitler's private apartments and the rest of the Old Chancellery.

Looking from the Wilhelmstraße (eastern) end, one was faced by a flight of steps almost as wide as the courtyard, leading up to a portal

Looking back to the east from outside the Anteroom doors, towards the Wilhelmstraße entrance – the view Hitler would have had while waiting to greet the most important of his visitors. On the left, an entrance led into the Siedler extension and thus to the Old Chancellery.

ABOVE AND ABOVE RIGHT: *'Partei' and 'Wehrmacht' statues by Breker.*

The doors leading from the Court of Honour into the Anteroom.

From this angle the two SS sentries guarding the entrance to the Anteroom show the scale of the Breker statues.

framed by four more columns. Greek- and Roman-style mythological figures were prominent in much of the decoration of this totalitarian nerve centre; flanking the steps on each side were two twice-lifesize bronze statues entitled 'Party' and 'Armed Forces', the work of Professor Arno Breker. (The fact that Hitler said that they were among the finest yet created in Germany perhaps tells us all we need to know about his taste.) The steps led up to a recessed bronze double door, set between two tall windows and below three others.

Surmounting the door was a bronze national emblem – the German eagle, this time with half-folded wings, again the work of Kurt Schmid-Ehmen; and in the bays of the porch ceiling above were panels of ornamental mosaics by Professor Hermann Kaspar.[51]

For illumination in the evenings lights had been built into the wall niches, to shine upwards and emphasize the structure of the building. In fact, the courtyard at night was like a black-and-white negative picture.

The architecture of the north and south façades of the Ehrenhof.

THE *VORHALLE* (ANTEROOM)

Once the visitor had passed through the Ehrenhof he ascended the steps of the portico flanked by Breker's two massive bronzes, and passed through the doors into a modest, almost homely room decorated with fresh flowers.

This Anteroom was rectangular, smaller and lower-ceilinged than the adjoining chambers; nevertheless, it still measured 17m wide by 10m long, and had a height of 7.5m (55ft 9in by 32ft 9in by 25ft 5in high). In the north and south walls doors gave access to the State Dining Room and to the upper office floors of the East wing, respectively. On each side of the door leading to the dining room, side doors gave access to a lift/elevator on the left and a staircase on the right. The tall, slender doors that connected the Vorhalle with the Ehrenhof were constructed from strong bronze sheeting; those opposite them on the west, leading to the Mosaiksaal, were made of mahogany.

The famous light red Untersberg marble, quarried near Salzburg, was used for the wall facings and mouldings. The floor of dark red Saalburg marble was covered centrally with a richly coloured carpet. In accordance with its character, the room contained little furniture other than chairs with light-coloured damask upholstery, and a 3m-long table with fine marble inlay. The artificial lighting came from bronze wall-sconces, and daylight entered through the two tall windows flanking the door leading out to the Ehrenhof.

The Anteroom, looking south. The entrance from the Court of Honour is to the left, between two windows; to the right are the doors leading to the Mosaiksaal. *The doors in the south wall lead to offices, staircases, and to the eastern street entrance of Voss-Straße No.4.*

The mahogany double doors leading from the Anteroom into the Mosaiksaal.

THE *MOSAIKSAAL* (MOSAIC HALL)

The impression made on the visitor passing from the plain Anteroom through the west door into the Mosaic Hall was striking. Lit only by a huge, flat glass rooflight, this chamber contained neither carpets nor furniture, which gave it a Classical austerity.

The doors at the western end of the Mosaic Hall, leading to the Round Vestibule. The steps were used to overcome the difference in floor levels.

ABOVE AND BELOW: *Decorative motifs in the* Mosaiksaal.

The Mosaiksaal, *with its glass ceiling to the sky. The viewpoint is to the west; on the right are the doors leading to the Dining Room.*

The Mosaiksaal covered an area 46.2m long by 19.2m wide (154ft 2in by 62ft 11in), and rose 16m (52ft 6in) to the glass ceiling. The walls were finished with smooth marble facings up to a height of 13.5m (44ft 3in). Above this, the roof mouldings supporting the glass roof jutted out in multiple layers of fluting. The door recesses at the east and west ends were flanked by two pairs of columns.

The wall surfaces, recesses and columns were built with Rotgrau Schnöll, a patterned Austrian marble found in the Salzburg area. This material was distinguished by its beautiful dark-red colour mixed with patches of light grey. The particular impression made by the room was due to its lavish and novel use of mosaics. This technique, which took root in Germany during the 19th century, had been almost completely ignored during more recent decades, for lack of suitable commissions. There was rarely any justification for such enrichment of surfaces unless the architect had confidence that the result would be worthy of the materials and technique, and long-lasting. Albert Speer was just such an architect, and in designing

his building he gave mosaics a part to play which did full justice to their character.

Professor Kaspar had provided ten large surfaces measuring 8.4m tall by 2.7m wide (27ft 6in by 8ft 10in), with narrow strips between the marble mouldings. The mosaic base presented various dark red shades, enlivened by small glass tesserae. The ornamental motifs consisted of pairs of eagles, torches, foliate sprays and swags of drapery in light grey shades, picked out with small gold and other coloured tesserae. There were five of these great mosaic panels on the south side of the hall, and four on the north, where there was a central door leading to the State Dining Room.

The floor was laid with large slabs of Saalburg marble separated by ornamental strips of marble and gold mosaic, and was edged with a broad band in a kind of double key pattern. The hall received natural light through the glass roof; artificial lighting was provided by elements above the glass, and indirectly by lights positioned behind bronze grills in the roof mouldings. Two more great bronze eagles by Schmid-Ehmen surmounted the end doors.

ABOVE: *The skylight reflected in the highly polished marble floor, the floor panels edged and separated by mosaic bands in repeat patterns.*

RIGHT: *Detail of one of the eagle-heads, removed after the war and restored within a new frame of white tesserae. (© Deutsches Historisches Museum Berlin)*

LEFT: *The decorative marble facing panels used on the north and south walls of the Mosaic Hall.*

THE *RUNDER SAAL* (ROUND VESTIBULE)

The Runder Saal was designed to overcome the difference in angle between the previous rooms and the Marmorgalerie that followed it to the west.

The domed roof was also the work of Hermann Kaspar; its pale-coloured finish gave it such a light, free appearance that the visitor was scarcely aware of it at all. The central skylight, at a height of 16m (52ft 6in) above the floor, was set in a broad, moulded bronze ring. The artificial lighting was provided indirectly through fittings inserted into recesses at the top of the walls, to illuminate the pale vaulting of the dome. Again, there were artificial lights above the skylight so that the room was always illuminated from the same apparent source, preserving the effect of the architecture by evening as by day.

The walls were faced with marble up to a height of 10.5m (34ft 5in); they were divided into eight sections, in two of which were located the doors on the longitudinal axis. Another section contained a smaller door leading to the administrative wing, and large statues by Arno Breker stood in front of the five remaining sections (see page 102). The marble used in this room was of two types, juxtaposing the dark red with the lighter stone quarried at Adnet in Austria; this involved a special technique known as incrustation. The floor of this room, 14.25m (46ft 9in) in diameter, was decorated with a mosaic devised by Hermann Kaspar.

The Runder Saal, *looking from west-to-east at the doors leading from the* Mosaiksaal.

A view across the Round Vestibule from east to west, to the doors into the Marmorgalerie. *Note that in these photos the five large statues by Breker are currently absent.*

The relief panels surmounting the doors: a female figure carrying a Roman standard above the east door from the Mosaiksaal, *and a male figure carrying a Roman sword above the west door leading to the* Marmorgalerie.

The cupola of the Round Vestibule.

Detail of the marble facings on the walls, and the patterned band round the edge of the floor.

THE *MARMORGALERIE* (MARBLE GALLERY)

From the domed vestibule the visitor entered the Marmorgalerie, which continued the east-to-west sequence. Here Albert Speer resurrected and gave a new meaning to a form of architecture for which there had no longer appeared to be any place. Although this was basically a communicating area it was, above all, the climax of the room sequence – the area leading immediately to the Führer's Study.

In terms of lavishness of design the Marmorgalerie of the New Reichs Chancellery was its most impressive space; it was no less than 146m (479ft) in length, with a breadth of 12m (39ft 4in) and a height of 9.5m (31ft), and it ran the whole length of the Mittelbau section of the building. A mirror-bright floor made of Saalburg Altrot marble extended over the whole surface. The walls were faced with light-coloured marble slabs, giving the gallery an unrestricted and splendid lightness and providing a most effective background for the colours of the furnishings and tapestries.

The gallery was furnished with tables, chairs, sofas and chests, all designed by Albert Speer himself.

A view westwards along the 146m (479-foot) length of the Marmorgalerie. *The central door of the five along the north wall led into Hitler's study.*

The central heating was concealed behind elegant brass and copper grilles.

Along the street (southern) side were spaced 19 tall windows, strongly profiled and surrounded by a dark red marble known as Deutschrot. The soffit depth of each window was 2.1m (6ft 10½in), so that the deep window recesses made a striking accompaniment to the surrounding frames along the whole length of the gallery. The windows themselves, which were 6m high and 2.35m wide (19ft 8in by 7ft 8½in), consisted of frosted panes with bronze glazing bars.

Opposite, spaced along the north side, stood five doors with massive surrounds of the same Deutschrot marble. The middle door led into the

Führer's Study and was crowned with a monogrammed 'AH' shield; the other doors, which led to the corridors in front of the adjutants' rooms, were surmounted by similar shields bearing coats-of-arms, all the work of the sculptor Hans Vogel. Above the doors leading to the Round Vestibule to the east and the Great Reception Hall to the west were two more of Kurt Schmid-Ehmen's eagle-and-swastika emblems.[52] Wall lamps with gilded bronze fittings gave the room a festive character, while lights built into the window surrounds radiated additional light from the same direction as the natural daylight.

Two SS sentries standing guard in the gallery at the doors to Hitler's study. Note that they stand on mats, to protect the floor from their boots and rifle butts.

Looking eastwards from the Marmorgalerie *through the door through which visitors entered the gallery from the* Runder Saal.

The gallery was furnished with tables, chairs, sofas and chests of drawers, all designed by Speer himself and decorated with striking marquetry and upholstery. The Marmorgalerie's pale marble was set off by this range of lively and beautiful colours; groups of furniture were arranged on carpets spread between the doors in the north wall, beneath great hanging tapestries – the Alexander series, chosen from the Vienna State Art History Museum. The room's splendid colour effects were further intensified by the choice of fresh flowers and foliage.

The south side of the gallery, showing some of the 19 deep window recesses.

THE *ARBEITZIMMER DES FÜHRERS* (HITLER'S STUDY)

Hitler's study looked out to the garden terrace outside the north wall through five French windows 6m high and 2m wide (19ft 8in by 6ft 6in). Five similar bays balanced the windows on the opposite wall, constructed with fine inlaid panels. In the middle bay on this south side was the entrance door leading in from the Marmor-galerie. There were two more doors in each of the end walls; these led into the corridors where the adjutants' offices were located, and (on the west) then to the State Cabinet Room.

The study measured 27m long by 14.5m wide (88ft 6in by 48ft 7in). The walls were covered with a dark red marble from Austria known as Lim-

The north-west corner of the study, with Hitler's desk. The doors behind it led via a corridor past adjutants' offices to the State Cabinet Room.

Hitler's desk (below), with details of the marquetry panels along the front (from top to bottom: Athena; Mars; Medusa).

The tapestry and chest on the west wall, beside the door leading to an adjutants' corridor and the State Cabinet Room. The tapestry was one of eight showing episodes from the myth of Dido and Aeneas, made in Antwerp in the 17th century by Wauters from cartoons by Giovanni Francesco Romanelli. It is not known where in the Chancellery the other seven were displayed.

bacher. At a height of 9.75m (32ft) was a coffered ceiling, the beams of darker wood than the recessed panels. The floor of Ruhpolding marble was covered with a single large reddish-brown carpet in a squared pattern with swastika motifs; large oriental rugs lay over this under Hitler's desk and the furniture by the fireplace at the eastern end.

The furnishings and layout were devised to be completely subordinate to the main spatial effects. In the east wall a fireplace measuring 2.7m high and 3.25m wide (8ft 10in by 10ft 8in) was built of the same marble as the walls; for this, Richard Klein had designed five cast-iron fire-back panels with pseudo-Classical figurative reliefs. The shields above the side doors were also the work of Richard Klein, while the national emblem above the entrance door, which was made of carved and gilded wood, was again by Kurt Schmid-Ehmen.

Albert Speer himself designed furniture for this room: Hitler's big writing desk, with its front incorporating three marquetry panels by Kaspar representing (from left to right) the heads of Athena, Mars and Medusa; the credenza unit on the west wall; and the large map table in front of the central window. This table consisted of an especially fine piece of Austrian marble, quarried and dressed as a single slab measuring 5m by 1.6m

Detail of the central marquetry panel on the chest beneath the tapestry on the west wall.

A view of the study looking to the south-east from behind Hitler's desk, with daylight from the French windows on the left; surmounted by an eagle on the right are the doors from the Marble Gallery. It was said that the lights were always burning in Hitler's studies – but what the Führer lacked was the energy to actually work. Meissner, Lammers, Bormann and the adjutants did most of the day-to-day work of government; in this study it was almost impossible for Hitler even to answer the telephone without getting up and walking round his desk.

(16ft 5in by 5ft 3in); the pattern for the inlay work was designed by Hermann Kaspar. In front of the fireplace was a cluster of less formal furniture: a long sofa and two armchairs upholstered in a blue/grey-and-white pattern, and other wing chairs in pale cream upholstery. By the window to the left of these stood a large terrestrial globe. One of a series of eight 17th-century 'Dido and Aeneas' tapestries hung on the west wall, and above the fireplace at the east end Lenbach's famous portrait of Bismarck.

The basic colours of this room came from a combination of the brown shades of the wood and the red-brown of the marble; the fine materials used created a colour synthesis that was severe and filled with restrained strength. A sycophantic writer declared that 'one entered this room with a feeling of reverence, since the great creative spirit of the man who worked there consecrates the surroundings'. (In fact, as has been exhaustively documented, Hitler was a lazy sovereign, utterly unsystematic in his work and easily distracted, who left the great majority of the actual business of government to his henchmen.)

General and detailed views of the doors in the south wall leading from the Marble Gallery.

Looking from west to east along the length of the study, with the French windows in the north wall leading to the garden terrace. Note at the far end, to the left of the furniture in front of the fireplace, the large terrestrial globe. The coffered ceiling was made from contrasting shades of wood.

LEFT: *Albert Speer designed the large marble-topped table especially for the Führer's study. It stood in front of the central of the five French windows; with magnification it is just possible to distinguish, through the glass, the orangery at the north side of the garden. During the final siege of the Government District of Berlin in April 1945 the table was turned on its side with its marble top facing the window, to give cover to defenders.*

RIGHT: *The fireplace, with the Lenbach portrait of Bismarck brought over from the Old Chancellery.*

Detail of the marble-topped table, seen from the end.

The furniture in front of the fireplace at the eastern end of the study.

Two of the five cast-iron fireback plates, by Richard Klein.

THE *REICHSKABINETTSSAAL* (STATE CABINET ROOM)

From the Führer's Study, a door close to his desk gave access to a corridor leading westwards, past adjutants' rooms to the State Cabinet Room. This measured 19m long by 13.5m wide (62ft 4in by 44ft 4in), with a 6.5m (21ft 4in) ceiling of the same coffered effect as that in the study. Its walls were covered with large sections of figured wood panelling and banding in contrasting shades, the north wall being pierced by four windows over-looking the terrace. The floor was covered with an almost wall-to-wall oriental carpet with an overall pattern of blue and wine-red diamond panels. A long conference table filled the centre of the room, covered with a tasselled cloth in rose-pink damask-patterned fabric with swastika motifs and broad wine-red borders. The table was flanked by two dozen armchairs, upholstered in similar colours but ornamented with large eagle-and-swastika national emblems; these, made from designs prepared by Paul Ludwig Troost, had been brought over from the Old Chancellery.

Further decoration of the room was by means of paintings hung on the north, south and west walls, and a large tapestry on the east wall (see Chapter 7). At that end, between the window and the northern door, stood a large globe of the world, the twin of that which stood in the Führer's Study.

The Reichskabinettssaal, *looking towards the western end, showing the upholstery of the chairs, the tablecloth and the diamond-patterned oriental carpet in wine-red and blue.*

Detail of the upholstery of the chairs and the cloth on the cabinet table.

A view eastwards along the length of the Cabinet Room, showing the globe and tapestry.

The door at the western end of the State Cabinet Room leading into the Great Reception Hall.

The northern of the two doors at the east end of the room. The globe was the pair to that which stood in Hitler's study; in 1940 they became famous through the Charlie Chaplin film The Great Dictator.

THE *GROSSER EMPFANGSSAAL* (GREAT RECEPTION HALL)

The long east-to-west axis of the State Apartments terminated in the Great Reception Hall, access to which was through two doors in its eastern wall, leading from the Marble Gallery and the State Cabinet Room. This great open chamber was 24.5m long and 16.5m wide (80ft 5in by 54ft), with a ceiling 11.6m (38ft) high. The walls were finished with fine plaster in large plain panels of an off-white shade separated by white bands, which created a very light, airy effect. In the western wall four tall, deeply recessed windows gave onto a large patio outside; central heating vents were concealed by decorative grilles below these. The parquet floor was covered almost out to the walls by an immense carpet specially hand-loomed for the room. The eastern, northern and southern walls were hung with three large tapestries. Paintings were hung low above small groups of furniture in the corners, and all the chairs, couches and chests were arranged against the walls, leaving the huge expanse of the carpeted floor unencumbered.

The most eye-catching features in this room were two outstanding cut-glass chandeliers some 4m (13ft) tall. Albert Speer had provided the basic design, and they were made by the famous Viennese glasscutters Lobmeyr. In this huge, uncluttered space the effect of the candle-like lamp holders integrated with the cascade of glittering glass drops was breathtaking.

A view towards the north-east corner of the Great Reception Hall, and the door leading from the State Cabinet Room.

The east wall; the only decorations in the Great Reception Hall were tapestries and a few paintings.
Chairs, banquettes and sideboards stood along the south, east and north walls.

A general view of the room, looking towards the south-east corner.

The south-east corner, showing the door leading from the Marble Gallery.

General view of the west wall, with three of the four exterior windows, seen from the north-east corner of the room.

Detail of the furniture in the south-east corner.

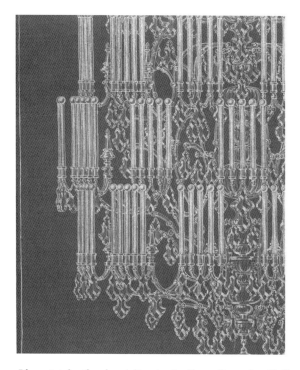

Blueprint for the chandeliers in the Great Reception Hall, prepared to a basic design by Speer, and a chandelier during assembly. (© Lobmeyr, Vienna)

Detailed and general views of one of the chandeliers. (© Lobmeyr, Vienna)

The decorative grille hiding one of the central heating vents under the windows in the west wall, which looked out over a large patio. See also details of the curtains, and the bronze glazing bars of the frosted glass window.

THE *SPEISESAAL* (DINING ROOM)

This was located on the north side of the East wing, with main access by doors from the Anteroom and Mosaic Hall. It was 48m long and 10.5m wide (157ft 6in by 34ft 5in), with a 5m (16ft 5in) ceiling. Like the Great Reception Hall, this long, rectangular saloon was finished in a pale colourscheme to compliment its airy atmosphere. It was lit during the day by 15 tall French windows and fanlights that occupied almost the whole northern wall, and gave access – via the colonnade – to the garden.

There were several entrances to the dining room. Up steps at the western end was a door that led via an adjutants' corridor towards the Führer's Study and the adjacent apartments; at the east, others led to corridors north of the Ehrenhof that led eventually to the Old Chancellery wing. At the western end of the south wall steps led up to an entrance into the Mosaic Hall, and at the eastern end others gave access to the Anteroom.

This pleasantly light room had something of the clean and unoppressive elegance of Paul Troost's work on ocean liners. There were no great central tables, but instead many individual tables each seating ten guests. The sole decorations in the room were paintings by Hermann Gradl.[54]

The 15 French windows along the north wall of the Dining Room gave access to the colonnade and the Chancellery garden beyond.

There were several entrances to the Dining Room; this one at the east end gave access from the Anteroom between the Court of Honour and the Mosaic Hall.

THE *BIBLIOTHEK* (LIBRARY)

This was situated on the first floor immediately above the dining room and the colonnade; it was 55.5m long by 7.4m wide (182ft by 24ft 3in). Along the north side recessed windows looked out over the garden; opposite these along the south wall were matching shallow niches, in which were placed large white porcelain urns from the Manufaktur Nymphenburg. Recessed into the panelled walls were glass-fronted cedarwood bookcases rising to 5m (16ft 5in). The floor was covered with a wall-to-wall carpet designed by Troost, with a pattern of stylized swastikas.

The vaulted ceiling rose to a maximum height of 7m (23ft), and it had been planned that it should be painted by Hermann Kaspar with allegorical scenes, but in fact these were never completed. Before the war put a stop to the work he did manage to finish several, representing such subjects as Music, Theatre and Astronomy.

Doors led from the Library into a large apartment known as the Model Room, 49m long by 6.77m wide (160ft 9in by 22ft 2in), and lit by a glass overhead cupola. This room housed the scale models for the Germania and Linz city redevelopment projects.

One of the large white porcelain Nymphenburg urns that stood in shallow niches along the south wall of the Library opposite the windows. The contents of the Library would be moved to the bunkers under the Chancellery in autumn 1940, at the very start of the RAF air raids. By summer 1943 the Secretary of State's library had been moved from the top floor of the East wing administrative quarters into the vacated Führer's Library.

The door to the Model Room.

The Library, looking towards the east; on the left are the windows in the north wall overlooking the Chancellery garden.

6   The Administrative Quarters, and Hitler's Private Apartments

The West (left) wing of the New Chancellery housed the administrative offices, together with those of Reichsminister Dr Lammers and his Reich Chancellery staff. On the upper floor of the Mittelbau block were the offices of the Party Chancellery under Reichsleiter Bouhler. The East wing was taken over by Staatsminister Dr Meissner with his staff of the Presidential Chancellery; the military adjutants also had their offices in this right wing.

Although they were not public spaces, great attention was given to the design, decoration and furnishing of all these areas. Each staircase, corridor, office and waiting room was constructed and equipped with the same degree of care; there were no neglected corners anywhere in the New Chancellery building.

Even in the 'practical' rather than 'ceremonial' areas of the Chancellery the architecture was monumental, in a pastiche of the styles of Classical or Egyptian temples.

Entrance hall in the East wing, Voss-Straße No.4, with corridor leading to the Presidential Chancellery.

Waiting rooms for visitors to the Old Chancellery; above, decorated with tapestries, is the waiting room for Hitler's study. (© Ullstein: 00781857 & 00781858)

A corridor and a conference room in the East wing of the Chancellery.

Stairs in a corridor connecting the East wing of the New Chancellery with Hitler's private apartments in the Old Chancellery.

A perspective view; this corridor in Voss-Straße No.2 gave access to the Presidential Chancellery, the domain of Staatsminister Dr Meissner.

A corridor in the West wing, Voss-Straße No.6.

Another angle on the glass-roofed entrance hall.

The study of Hitler's chief personal adjutant from 1934 to 1940, Wilhelm Brückner.
(© Ullstein: 00781856)

Dr Meissner's office in the East wing.

HITLER'S PRIVATE APARTMENTS

Hitler was finally able to take up residence in the (Old) Reichs Chancellery at Wilhelmstraße No.77 in May 1934. As described in Chapter 2, he found it unsatisfactory, and this applied not only to the public rooms and offices. Nevertheless, his private quarters would remain in this wing even after the construction of the New Chancellery.

Shortly after his rise to power in 1933, Hitler spent several hours surveying the old Chancellery together with his favourite architect from Munich, Paul Ludwig Troost; somewhat later he also showed Albert Speer around the old building. Paint was peeling off walls, and a smell of decay permeated everything; the kitchen had no direct sunlight and its facilities were seriously out of date; there was only a single bathroom, and that dated back to the turn of the century. Hitler became increasingly agitated during his tour with Troost, and is reported to have said that he would be embarrassed to receive even a single foreign visitor in these premises.

Hitler's private apartments were located to the right (north) side of the large reception room on the first floor.[55] Traudl Junge, Hitler's secretary, reported that Hitler boasted that he had saved this hall by having a new floor and ceiling installed; he repeated his tale about 'the old man' (Hindenburg) warning him about the unsafe state of the floors when he arrived to be sworn in as Reich Chancellor. Traudl Junge remembered the Old Chancellery as a curious warren that remained impractical and awkward even after its refurbishment: 'There were so many staircases, service staircases, halls, doors and antechambers that the whole complex was nothing short of a labyrinth. It took quite a while before I could find my way around.'

Hitler's private rooms overlooked the park behind the Old Chancellery. The apartment, with its monumental double doors, contained a private study, a living room with library, a bedroom with en-suite bathroom, and a dressing room that would later be transformed by Eva Braun into a boudoir. Both windows in Hitler's bedroom overlooked the park of the Reichs Chancellery, while

Reception room in the Führer's private apartments in the Old Chancellery. (© Ullstein: 00097261)

a door led to a private terrace that had been partly transformed into a roof garden. Beneath this terrace lay the dining room, next to the Wintergarten (conservatory). The living room/library contained a fireplace, though it was used less frequently than that in the salon on the floor below.

The living room was also used to display the numerous gifts that Hitler was accustomed to hand around at Christmas to friends and those close to him – men and women who worked closely with him and their spouses, but also artists he admired, actors and actresses, as well as old friends from the early days of the NSDAP. According to Christa Schroeder, Hitler regretted his lack of time to shop for these presents. To make sure he had some personal input into the choosing of gifts, the *Hausintendant* (majordomo or butler) Artur Kannenberg arranged for the most exclusive Berlin shops to deliver a selection of their wares to the Chancellery. These were then spread over all available tables, chairs, and even on the floor of the living room and the adjacent private study. A long list of names determined who was to receive a gift from Hitler that year; this list was carefully maintained by his chief adjutant Julius Schaub, who also made a note of the gifts given to the people on the list in previous years.

'Willi' Kannenberg – a short, rotund, somewhat clownish figure (who played the accordion) – ruled over the Hitler household like a sheik. Those in his favour could always count on a steady supply of coffee, chocolate, and other normally rationed or unobtainable treats, which he served in his small 'private tavern' at any hour of the day or night. His wife, Frieda, was a modest, quiet, even-tempered woman, complimented by Hitler as a model for the perfect German *Hausfrau*. She knew exactly what Hitler's tastes were in floral and table decorations, which she ordered from the most expensive florist in Berlin. Frau Kannenberg even knew exactly how to use flowers and other decorations to lighten up the gloomy, museum-like atmosphere that hung in most of the larger halls of the Chancellery; she made sure that the colours of the flowers were in harmony with the surrounding paintings.

Hitler's private apartments could be reached by a large staircase that gave onto a spacious hall with red velvet carpeting. Through a large double door, one entered Hitler's private living room; Eva Braun's personal boudoir could also be reached from the large entrance hall. Straight across from the living room was a door that led to a long corridor of Hitler's personal adjutants' quarters, located in the right wing of the Old Chancellery. Beside these adjutants, Reich Press Chief Dr Otto Dietrich, SS General 'Sepp' Dietrich (chief of the Leibstandarte-SS regiment that provided the ceremonial sentries), various secretaries, and Drs Brandt, von Hasselbach, Haase and Morell were also stationed in this wing. The court photographer Heinrich Hoffmann also had his room there, as did the SD bodyguard Rochus Misch.

At the beginning of the adjutants' corridor was a small room with a view onto the small courtyard between the Old Chancellery and the Foreign Ministry to the north; this room was occupied by Hitler's valets.[56] On the opposite side, beyond a few steps leading down to a lower floor-level and right behind the stairwell, was the so called Stairwell Room (*Treppenzimmer*). Both Hitler and his secretaries used this room to catch their breath when necessary; it was modestly furnished, with a very high ceiling and only one window, overlooking the lawn of the Old Chancellery. It was originally intended as a sort of emergency spare bedroom, since it also had a simple washbasin with a mirror.

Even after the New Chancellery had been completed in 1939, Hitler spent most of his time in or around his private quarters on the first floor of the old building. So that they could be as close to him as possible his secretaries used the stairwell as a central axis, and the small Stairwell Room for taking refreshment; the butler Kannenberg made sure fresh bread rolls were always available there, as well as fresh coffee, tea, soft drinks and a large bowl of fruit. According to secretary Christa Schroeder, Hitler had the habit of walking in unannounced and asking the ladies if he could join them, often staying for an hour or so.

Left of the large entrance hall to Hitler's private apartments was the breakfast room. He did not use this much, but it also gave access to his study

Adjutants' corridor, giving access to Hitler's private study in the Old Chancellery.
(© Ullstein: 00781854)

on one side and the former Congress Hall on the other. During the war Hitler would reach the Congress Hall from his study via the breakfast room, to join his military staff for their daily military situation reports.

To the left of the Congress Hall were four rooms for his adjutants and secretaries and a waiting room for guests. Next to these was Hitler's official study in the Old Chancellery, the 'Red Room'.

On the ground floor of the Old Chancellery was a mixture of smaller rooms and State rooms. In general, visitors arrived via a large vestibule. Immediately opposite the entrance were two high doors that gave access to a large reception hall with a fireplace, where Hitler used to receive his guests. To the right of it were the music room, smoking room, and the dining room that gave access to the Wintergarten.

In the evenings the music room was also used to show films, and the smoking room was the gathering-place for guests invited for lunch or supper. After a film screening Hitler liked to retire to this room with his guests, to end the day gath-ered together around the fireplace (needless to say, the 'smoking' room was never used for that purpose – the Führer was well known to be a fanatical anti-smoker). From the smoking salon, one entered the dining room with the adjacent conservatory. The latter was added in 1935, and was actually quite a large and luxurious reception room. To the right side of this were large glass doors leading to a large and magnificent chamber with dark marble columns, known as the Hall of Diplomats; this, too, was a later addition, and used solely for state banquets and receptions. The reception hall's main architectural feature was a large wall containing high glass doors, giving onto the extensive terrace.

During the day the Wintergarten was Hitler's favourite room; there he would hold meetings and, weather permitting, he would entertain guests – his closest collaborators, and during the war senior military commanders – out on the terrace for hours. The conservatory also served as breakfast room; to the left of it were several smaller rooms used by Hitler's cooks, the Kannenbergs, and valets.

7   Works of Art
    in the Chancellery

Speer's Reichs Chancellery was a building designed not only to impose a sense of Germany's power on visiting heads of state or ambassadors; it was also meant to be a showroom for German artistic craftsmanship. The architecture and materials of the structure itself answered this purpose, as did its carpets, furniture, paintings, statues and every other element of its decoration and furnishing.

Propaganda Minister Goebbels spread the message that the New Chancellery would become the exemplar of art in the new Germany. German magazines and newspapers of the period – among them *Kunst dem Volk, Völkisher Beobachter, Das Reich, Kunst im Dritten (Deutsches) Reich* – devoted page after page to the building and the associated craftsmanship. Special-edition books were published, and frequently given as presents

Marquetry design used on furniture.

A chest and a chair in the Marble Gallery.

to the Führer's official visitors. In those years huge numbers of people visited cinemas at least once a week, and the Chancellery was revealed to the German public in the weekly newsreels of *Die Deutsche Wöchenschau.*

With miles of corridors, hundreds of rooms and many state chambers, the decoration and furnishing of the building was a major and time-consuming aspect of the overall project.

Each of the state rooms received its own specially designed furniture, but without sacrificing the unifying overall style designed by Albert Speer. The inlay and marquetry designs were by Hermann Kaspar, the creator of the Mosaic Hall. The furniture was manufactured by the Vereinigte Werkstätten für Kunst im Handwerk AG (United Workshops for Art in Handicraft). For example, for the chests of drawers in the Marble Gallery they used softwood veneered with walnut, maple, Amboyna burl and rosewood, while the chairs were made of beechwood in the same colours as the chests.

The Vereinigte Werkstätten had been founded in Munich in 1898 and quickly became one of the leading enterprises in German interior design and furnishing. Their portfolio listed furniture and craft objects by Richard Riemerschmid, Rudolf Alexander Schröder, Bruno Paul and Paul Ludwig Troost. The Workshops' close relations with the Troost studio, which gave major impulses to the architecture and interior design of the Third Reich, ensured that the Vereinigte Werkstätten became the dominant company in its field during the 1930s. Apart from the Old and New Chancelleries, the Workshops were commissioned to provide furniture for clients such as the Propaganda and Foreign ministries, the German Embassy in London, Göring's huge hunting-lodge Karinhall, the Führerbau and the NSDAP administration building in Munich, and Hitler's residence on the Obersalzberg.

Since the New Chancellery was to be a stage-set for performances to awe both German and foreign audiences, the lighting was equally important. Most of the state rooms, with the exception of the Great Reception Hall, were lit by means of bronze wall fittings and indirect light from glass ceilings or hidden niches in the walls.

As illustrated in Chapter 5, for the Grosser Empfangssaal two giant chandeliers were commissioned from the renowned Viennese company of Lobmeyr. In 1936 the owner of the firm was forced to give up his position because he was unable to produce the 'Grosse Ariernachweis' – the document required under the Nazi race laws to confirm that owners of certain types of business did not have an unacceptable proportion of Jewish blood among the past two generations of their family. (The consequent forced sale of many art and antiques dealerships and much stock in 1935–36 caused a major slump in the market prices of such items.) However, his son Hans Harald Rath was able to satisfy the official requirements (presumably having no more than one Jewish grandparent out of the four), and he was able to take over the company in his father's place. Hans Harald Rath and Speer were of similar opinions in the matter of quality and craftsmanship, and it was this, rather than any

political sympathies, that secured Lobmeyr the the order to make the chandeliers.[57]

One of the inheritances that Speer adopted from Professor Troost was the use of mosaics. The Emperor Wilhelm II had always seen it as a way to express his imperial dignity and semi-divine rights, but since the downfall of the last Kaiser in 1918 this ancient method of decorating churches, monuments and other public buildings had lost much of its popularity. Troost had started to use mosaics for National Socialist projects like the Braunhaus in Munich, and Speer followed his example, employing this technique extensively in the New Reichs Chancellery – in particular, of course, in the immense 900 square metre (9,700sq/ft) Mosaiksaal. Mosaics were used to demonstrate power by the association of Nazi with ancient symbols – swastikas in combination with eagles, torches and laurels. Other examples of this craft were to be found on the terrace in front of Hitler's study and at both main entrances in Voss-Straße.

The Führer's Study, the State Cabinet Room and the Great Reception Hall were all embellished with 16th, 17th and 18th century canvases, most of them from the State Art Historical Museum in Vienna and the Fine Arts Museum in Berlin. Hitler was a man of limited and pedestrian artistic taste, and the choice of paintings to hang in the New Chancellery was more influenced by their decorative aspect than their true merit. Some were quite unremarkable; more interestingly, however, others were in surprising violation of Party ideology. For example, the most important work of art in the State Cabinet Room was a Tintoretto depicting the Biblical scene of Moses being found in the bullrushes by Pharaoh's daughter. Presumably the men who sat around the long table were completely unaware that they were being overlooked every day by a scene from the life of one of the central figures in Jewish religious history.

The walls of the State Dining Room were decorated with paintings by the Nuremberg artist Hermann Gradl.[58] A painter of idyllic landscapes, Gradl had only been working on small to medium-sized canvases when he was commissioned by Hitler to design and complete six monumental paintings for the dining room. Hitler did not think Gradl simply an important German landscape artist; he even declared that he was one of the 12 most important artists in the Third Reich. Gradl was therefore invited to join the Führer at the celebration of his 50th birthday in Berlin. On 23 May 1939 the painter received a down payment of 70,000RM so he could commence work on the six large paintings; five of the commissioned subjects were 'Mountaintops', 'Small Brook', 'Marine Landscape', 'Lowlands' and 'Floodlands', illustrating the 'typical appearance of the German Land, in its intertwining of Nature and Culture, and its many different guises as Motherland of the German Nation'. When the state finally received the paintings on 10 May 1941, Gradl was paid the remainder of the

120,000RM fee. Whether or not all of them were completed, and what happened to them, remains unknown. Hitler himself did at one point buy an oil painting entitled 'Landscape with the River Main', for the sum of 23,000 Reichmarks.

Other recent works in the heavy new 'National Socialist style' were also acquired, and many were bought by Hitler personally at exhibitions in the Haus der Deutschen Kunst. At one time he bought 144 contemporary works of art to decorate the Chancellery, for a total of 367,530RM; in 1942, on Albert Speer's advice, he bought another 180 contemporary paintings.

A month before the New Chancellery was due to be handed over to the Führer in 1939, Albert Speer and two employees from the Berlin carpet-makers Quantmeyer und Eicke were flown to

Two of Arno Breker's bronze statues for the Runder Saal.

Vienna in a specially chartered plane in order to make a selection of art for the Chancellery. All these objects were provided 'on loan'; they were of genuine artistic and historical value, such as the paintings by Angelika Kaufmann acquired by the Emperor Josef II.[59]

The reason that two staff members of a carpet company accompanied Speer to Vienna was that the huge, empty walls of the Chancellery cried out for the display of tapestries. Together with the use of mosaics, these were to lend an air of antique importance to the interior. The artist Werner Peiner was commissioned to make a series of eight cartoons for tapestries intended for the Marmorgalerie, showing the fateful battles of German history, but in 1940 only six of the eight studies were ready.[60] As early as 1938 the Art Historical Museum in Vienna was informed that it would be required to let Speer have three series of tapestries for the Chancellery 'on temporary loan', and these were selected by Speer and the people from Quantmeyer und Eicke during their trip; the receipts for them are dated 27 February 1939. These series consisted of:

Eight 17th-century Dutch tapestries depicting scenes from the life of Alexander the Great, following Charles Le Brun's paintings and the cartoons made after them in Paris.

Five 17th-century Brussels tapestries showing scenes from the life of the Roman hero Decius Mus, after cartoons by Rubens.

Eight 17th-century Antwerp tapestries showing episodes from the lives of Dido and Aeneas, by M. Wauters following cartoons by Giovanni Francesco Romanelli.[61]

The appeal of the first series was obvious; the latter two illustrated figures symbolizing dedicated patriotism – Decius Mus on the field of battle, and Aeneas as the legendary founder of Rome, a nation destined to become rulers of the world.

The Alexander tapestries were all of different sizes, ranging from 4.15m by 8.1m (13ft 7in by 26ft 6in) to 4.15m by 2.9m (13ft 7in by 9ft 6 inches). The new ones designed by Peiner all measured 5.4m by 10m (17ft 8in by 32ft 9 inches). This made them hard to combine with the extreme and far-fetched symmetry of the Chancellery's rooms and corridors.

A tapestry above a banquette between two of the doors in the north wall of the Marble Gallery.

8   'How Adolf Hitler's Command Post Functions'

This article, written by Hubert Nunn and published in *Das Reich* on 6 April 1941, is, of course, entirely a work of Nazi propaganda rather than journalism, and every word certainly had to be passed by the censor. Much of it is fairly numbing 'boilerplate copy', churned out by an obedient hack. It is reprinted here in translation mainly to show what the German public were being told at that date, but even the obvious propaganda of the early passages has some historical interest (from the lies that were being told, we can judge some of the subjects that the German people were not supposed to be thinking about).

Readers may be surprised by the picture Nunn paints of the functions actually performed in the nominal government headquarters of a major power in wartime. This emphasizes the essential nature of the Nazi state: the machinery of checks and balances had been dismantled, and all major decisions were being made elsewhere – often arbitrarily, without co-ordination, and indeed in direct competition.

Two imposing portals, countless rows of windows, an impressively looming facade. Soldiers stand in front of square columns, SS to the left, Wehrmacht to the right. One only notices them as they salute a passing officer; otherwise, they fade into the stone-grey background. It's as if the street was made up of just this one building; the older houses on the opposite side seem strangely out of time and place. Even traffic seems to fade away. Only further on, on Wilhelmplatz and in Hermann-Göring-Straße, do cars and carriages roll past in close file.

The front of the New Reichs Chancellery is over 400 meters wide. Nobody could walk past it without wondering what goes on inside. A mysterious veil seems to shroud such buildings. And in these days, when all power has been handed over to a small group of leaders, that mystery seems enhanced. Gone are the days when noisy parliamentarians made a public spectacle of the fruitless planning and scheming of the government. Today, plans and schemes have made place for action and decisions, which show the proper work of the Reich's leaders. The inner workings of the government are kept discreetly from prying eyes. The number of people involved in turning abstract plans into concrete actions is therefore rather limited.

However, the civil servants in their brown liveries, waiting behind the heavy double doors, know these men more than well. They know their faces and demeanour; they know which one seldom speaks, and which one is friendly. Every person holding an important post in the government walks these halls and asks these servants for directions and information, or gives them tasks and advice. Sometimes, there are just three generals' coats hanging on the racks in the waiting room. At other times it's the uniforms of the Reich's leaders, SA commanders, Gauleiters or troop inspectors. At times, civilians may hang their coats here. But the overcoat being brought in right now belongs to Dr Schacht.

Without a sound, the elevator cages open automatically as the gates close. Unfalteringly, guards step forward, asking for visitor's permits. Slowly, the eye adjusts itself to the unusual size of things, that ever-surprising hallmark of Speer's architecture. That feeling of oppression, enhanced by the deliberate dimensions of the corridors, seems to fade away. Slowly, one is able to regain one's bear-

A brown-uniformed clerk in one of the corridors of the Chancellery. The yellow sign with a red arrow indicates the direction of the nearest accessible air raid shelter.
(© Ullstein Bild)

Cleaning ladies vacuuming and dusting in a 'State Council Room'; while similar, details of the decor suggest that this is not the State Cabinet Room.
(© Ullstein Bild)

ings. And what seemed impossible during a first visit, now slowly becomes second nature: that natural instinct for direction, the feeling for distance between point of departure and destination. With a steadier tread, one walks across the thick carpets that seem to dampen every sound. The yellow signs pointing towards air raid shelters no longer seem to trouble you.

Three departments hold court in over 400 rooms. The Reich Chancellery takes up most of the left wing; the NSDAP Führer's Chancellery is located in the upper floor of the central building; and finally the Presidential Chancellery, reached through the right-hand doors. Most of the ground floor of the central building is reserved for state rooms: the reception hall, the circular hall, the hall of mosaics and last but not least the marble gallery, which contains the entrance to the

Führer's official workroom. Most of these are seldom used, even the Führer's workroom is reserved just for special occasions. On normal working days Adolf Hitler is to be found at home, in the old Reich Chancellor's Palace, which can be seen from certain windows, lying beyond the garden.

The day moves at a quick pace. Civil servants scurry up and down stairwells, clutching file folders under their arms. Cleaning ladies keep countless vacuum cleaners purring, while a worker kneels, repairing a weakened spot in the marble floor.

The history of the Chancellery goes back almost 70 years. When Bismarck's original state function – that of Reich Chancellor, responsible for all central affairs of state – was slowly split up into separate functions (the forerunners of the current

Reich ministers), he found himself without a central bureau that could deal with his own interests as Chancellor. So, on 18 May 1878, a special secretariat was created, which was given the name of Reich Chancellery. A special council was put in charge of this new secretariat. At the very beginning only a small number of administrative workers were sufficient to deal with its tasks.

During the following decades the original building was slowly expanded, and the number of civil servants grew steadily, while the office itself grew in lustre. From 1906 onwards an Under-Secretary was placed at its head. From 1920, a State Secretary replaced him, without changing the actual duties. The Chancellery itself held no special function. It merely served as a mediator between the Chancellor, his ministers, and the parliament.

Under Adolf Hitler, all this did not change much. The Chancellery's function was enlarged, and its influence made wider. A 'certain distance between the Chancellery and the Chancellor' was created. This means that it is no longer the Chancellor himself who is in charge of the Chancellery, but a 'Chief of the Reich Chancellery', who was appointed and elevated into the highest ranks of government even way back in 1934. Whereas former Chancellors were personally involved with the workings of the Chancellery, appointing and dismissing staff and personally receiving various parties, Reich Minister Dr Lammers now takes care of all these responsibilities. As such, he answers only to the Führer himself.

From out of this building, the Reich is being governed. Even when the Führer is not in Berlin, but in the Obersalzberg or in his Headquarters, the daily toil of governing the nation takes place in this building. A dedicated courier service ensures the necessary communications.

Daily government: that means all things relating to official state business and state government. When cleared of all ballast, every single thread leads to the green chambers of the Reich Minister. He separates the important from the inconsequential and brings together various related threads. Numerous different things must be taken into account, to ensure that this task is dealt with

professionally. Let's take a look at the large switchboard positioned next to Dr Lammer's desk. Even the names by the various buttons show the number of high-ranking people who are in close contact with the Chief of Government of our glorious German Reich. While formal gatherings of the Reich Cabinet are rather rare occurrences these days (the government has convened only 80 times since 1933), Adolf Hitler is continuously kept up to date with developments in major political issues (insofar as he has not been informed by responsible ministers, of course, which is often the case in matters of foreign policy). Of course, this does not include military matters, matters directly related to the Chief of State, or matters relating to the NSDAP.[62]

The actual number of civil servants and employees stands in stark contrast to the size of the building. Only about 70 people deal with all matters relating to the government. They are led by two Ministerial Directors, whose function is that of heads of department. Three Cabinet Councillors, three Ministerial Councillors, two Chief Government Councillors and two Government Councillors fill out the list of high officials. Fourteen Office Councillors, two Government Inspectors and five Chief Secretaries of the Presidential Chancellery are employed, along with a small number of clerks and typists in order to deal with additional work. The total number of people employed falls somewhere in the region of 250, most of whom are assigned to technical functions, such as messengers or maintenance men.

Both heads of department must report to the Führer; the head of Department A is also personal counsel to the Führer. The Reich Cabinet Councillors are charged with overseeing various matters entrusted to the ministerial councils. This only goes to show how intricately linked each councillor is to the whole field of operations of the Chancellery. This is no incidental development. Dr Lammers has spoken on various occasions against too strict a specialization of the councillors. He is convinced that a splintering of functions works against a healthy forward impulse. And experience has taught him that this impulse is exactly what is necessary for the proper functioning of the Chancellery. Every single one of his officials must be

The mail room of the New Chancellery. (© Ullstein Bild)

able to have a clear view of the greater picture, in order to solve specific problems and answer individual questions within a larger context.

Just as in any other big company, the first work of the day can be observed near the post entrance. When the postman, who has just left the post office at the nearby Leipziger-Straße, makes his early morning call at the mailroom on the second floor and puts his bag full of mail on the table, he sets in motion a chain of orders that come in from outside. Most of these letters and packages are registered mail, some even carry official seals.

In 1932 the number of incoming items of mail ran to 515,000. In 1933, this number increased by 70 per cent (close to 375,000 more items), only to fall back by 200,000 items the following year. The reason for this decrease can be clearly found in the flourishing economy: the number of letters begging for work has all but disappeared. Nevertheless, the volume is now stabilized at four times that of 1932.

Registering and handling this mail is done according to those methods that are now widespread in German industrial life. Each single item, however insignificant, is entered into a ledger, and when it can't be dealt with within the normal business of the Chancellery it is handed over to the relevant department without further ado. The sender is always notified of where his letter is, so that he can always inform himself about the course of his enquiry.

Next to official correspondence, a large pile of personal letters comes in every day. These contain personal grievances and private concerns from people all over the Reich, and even abroad. They often contain the most curious formulas. A glance

The Chancellery staff restaurant, on the ground floor at the corner of Hermann-Göring-Straße and Voss-Straße. (© Ullstein Bild)

at today's bundle: 'c/o the Secret Cabinet of the Führer'; 'c/o the Reich Government, more specifically the Führer'; 'To His Excellency, the Most Nobly Born Führer'; 'to Obersalzberg in Berlin'. This curious multitude of opinions and queries shows perfectly the unusual trust that the public at large place in Adolf Hitler. These days, a surprisingly large number of letters come from people in newly acquired or recently occupied territories, addressing the Führer himself. It can only be seen as significant that a large portion of the mail comes from abroad, and that it is mostly from foreigners who wish to pay their respects to the Führer.

Next to the Führer's offices are the official rooms of the Chief of the Reich Chancellery; the Chief of the Presidential Chancellery, State Minister Dr Meissner; and the Chief of the Chancellery of the NSDAP Führer, Reich leader Bouhler. Their adjutants can also be found in these rooms. These offices make up the general command post of Adolf Hitler, the instrument he uses to deal with all matters of government.

The Reichs Chancellery cannot be separated from the daily workings of the government. It is here that the matters currently concerning the Cabinet are dealt with. It is also here that the Führer makes his most important decisions. Within its walls, the Reich Ministers can work unhindered. Only when their work results in some consequence for the population in general – that is, when their work leads them to make new laws – are the other members of the cabinet informed by the Chief of the Reich Chancellery. Their opinions are taken into account, their questions are answered, and finally the approval and the signature of the Führer himself are secured.

It used to be custom that the Chief of the Reich Chancellery prepared Ministerial Councils and Cabinet meetings. This continues to this day. He is now also charged with organizing the meetings and briefings of the Secret Cabinet and the Reich Defence Council that was summoned at the onset of the war. This securely anchors the workings of the Chancellery within the bounds of the law-making offices. This has greatly facilitated the introduction of new laws. Instead of discussing proposals for laws in formal gatherings, ideas and designs for new laws are directly transmitted to the relevant ministers, who then have their say or exchange ideas about the proposal. On top of the large piles of documents that are worked through by employees of the Chancellery, one can see several thicker pieces of paper: typewritten drafts for new laws. They can easily be recognized by the Great Seal of the Reich, which is affixed to each one next to the signatures.

While appointing and dismissing civil servants is officially one of the duties of the Presidential Chancellery, the practical preparations for such matters are made within the Reich Chancellery. All that is left for the Chancellery of the Head of State is to make matters official. This form of centralization, however, means a significant increase in work. It might be interesting to note that Dr Lammers is also in charge of the Gratitude Gift Fund created on 17 February 1938.

The day marches on, couriers come and go. While the reception halls and state chambers are peacefully empty, the cabinet rooms of the Chancellery are overrun with activity. The war has led to an increase in activities, and has complicated the way in which these activities are conducted. Some of the rooms are not used on a daily basis. For example, the workroom of the President of the Secret Cabinet Council, Freiherr von Neurath, can be found in one of the wings of the building. In yet another one can find the bureau of the Reich Press Chief. Both have been furnished, in order to be ready for use on occasions that require the presence of the Führer himself in the Chancellery.

The longer one dwells in these halls, the more clearly one can form a picture of the inner work-

The office of Dr Otto Dietrich, State Press Chief. (© Ullstein Bild)

ings of this building. The architectural achievements of this modern building, which was constructed in a mere nine months, seem to become ever more impressive as a result of this deeper understanding. With every step, one comes to see how every single outward detail has been shaped to the utmost perfection, paralleling the inner structure and organization of the services employed within the building. A clear and uniform style dominates the interior. The State Cabinet Room is as much a harmonic part of the whole structure as the office of a civil servant. Every single room is part of a greater design.

To create this impression of being part of a larger whole was the main goal of this new building. In the single press article written by the Führer since he took control of the nation, Adolf Hitler described this ideal. In this article he also wrote about previous buildings: the Chancellery under Bismarck, and the building in the Wilhelmplatz, constructed during Brüning's reign. He pointed out how these buildings were inaccessible, clearly unfit to represent a world power. Today, these buildings have been absorbed by the new and far greater complex. The 1932 building, which was later fitted with a balcony, now serves as the guards' abode. Even the old Borsig Palace, situated at the corner of Voss-Straße and Wilhelm-straße, could be considered to form part of the new Chancellery. Though it isn't located within the premises of the New Chancellery, its functions clearly bind them together; it houses the offices of the Chief-of-Staff of the SA.

To round off our view of the Chancellery, it must be noted that Special Services have also been assigned to the Chancellery. These Special Services each fulfil some function that could not be assigned to an already existing service within the government. These include, amongst others, the Inspector General of German Roads, the Inspector General for the State Capital, and the Reich Commissioner for the Establishment of the German National Identity. All the recently appointed and newly created Reich Commissioners are also an integral part of the Chancellery.

A small camp bed is laid out for the night watch somewhere in a tiny room. The switchboard is manned 24 hours a day. Someone is present around the clock to receive and despatch orders. The buzz of activity never ceases. This activity is undoubtedly the most important within the

The switchboard in the telephone room of the New Chancellery. (© Ullstein Bild)

Reich: it captures all those different threads that govern the life of our community. What goes on behind the monumental facade in the Voss-Straße serves our Nation. Our Nation's people are its living substance, the element that inspires, moves and carries forward this unending activity.

9 History – the Reichs Chancellery at War

On Monday 9 January 1939, 24 hours earlier than planned, the New Reichs Chancellery was ready to be handed over to the Führer (though even after it was handed over to the state work still continued, into 1943).

After all the propaganda that had lauded German craftsmanship, claiming that this building would be superior to anything yet seen, the inauguration was marked by a series of gatherings and ceremonies in the presence of all who had participated in its construction. Due to bad weather, the intended open-air ceremony in the Ehrenhof at 10.45am could not take place and was hastily relocated to the Berlin Sports Palace. At 1.30pm, Speer officially handed over the building to the state, the ceremony being followed by a meal in the banqueting hall of the Berlin Zoo, and that evening by special theatre and variety shows. Hitler, accompanied by a small number of his immediate entourage, came to visit the building. Those who had assisted in its construction were also allowed to come and see the result of their work.

With the New Year reception approaching, the guard of honour rehearsed their drill in the Ehrenhof and outside opposite the gate in

The guard of honour, now uniformed in field-grey, drilling in the Ehrenhof.
(© Bundesarchiv: 101III – Wisniewski 003-29)

Wilhelmstraße. Chancellery chauffeurs practised the clockwise method of entering and leaving the courtyard. Traffic lights, to halt the street traffic when cars were entering or leaving the Chancellery, were tested.

On 12 January 1939 the entire Berlin *corps diplomatique* were received in the New Chancellery. When each of the 52 foreign diplomats drove in from Wilhelmstraße through the huge bronze doors of the Ehrenhof, a company of the guard of honour presented arms. Climbing the staircase in front of the doors leading into the Anteroom, they were received by the master of ceremonies of the Foreign Ministry, Freiherr Alexander von Dörnberg. Once inside they were helped by servants dressed in blue coats with silver braid, red vests and black silk knee-breeches.

Anticipating the moment, Hitler had said: 'When these gentlemen enter the Mosaic Hall they must immediately sense the whole sublime nature of the Greater German Reich. The long corridors will reduce my visitors to humility.' Now was the time to test it. From the Mosaic Hall, Chief of the Presidential Chancellery Meissner and Freiherr von Dörnberg guided them along the Marble Gallery to the Great Reception Hall. Here Hitler and the doyen of the diplomatic corps in Berlin, the Papal Nuncio Cesare Orsenigo, exchanged speeches.

Indeed, the new building impressed those who had been invited. On Monday 23 January 1939, *Time Magazine* published an article simply entitled 'A.H.', describing the New Year diplomatic reception and the architecture of the New Chancellery:

Good enough for German Chancellors before Adolf Hitler was the modest, graceful little Chancellery with its tree-shaded entrance on Berlin's Wilhelmstraße. As the office and official residence of the head of the Third Reich, however, the little building has long been considered inadequate. Some time ago the Führer commissioned his favourite architect, 33-year-old Albert Speer, designer of many Nazi Party buildings at Nürnberg and co-planner, with Architect Hitler, of the ambitious Nazi project to rebuild

Berlin,* to draw up plans for a Chancellery which would serve as a monument to its Nazi builders.

A year ago workmen began to raise an entire block of buildings on Vosstraße, running from Wilhelmstraße to Hermann Göringstraße, near the old Chancellery. Some 6,000 labourers went to work in night and day shifts to erect the building in record time. At Christmas the Führer called them together, presented each with a prized package of sausage, bacon, lard and coffee, and spurred them to complete the structure in time for his annual reception of the diplomatic corps. They did.

As diplomats from 52 nations arrived last week they saw a block-long (1,400 ft), three-storey structure, covered with yellow-tinted stucco, trimmed with grey stone. It consists of three main parts: two huge wings, housing some 400 administrative offices of the vast Nazi bureaucracy, and a central section, which contains the Führer's office and the vast Long Hall. Elsewhere in the building are his private quarters, official reception galleries, a huge library and a room filled with models of buildings planned for the beautification of Berlin. The German press acclaimed the architectural style as 'severely classic.' Foreign observers were less kind. They described its appearance as 'militant,' a 'barracks.'

Inside, the diplomats found the building more imposing. The room they were most eager to see was the Führer's private office. Its door, surmounted by a heavy bronze shield bearing the monogram 'A.H.,' was guarded by two armed, black-shirted Elite Guards. When the door swung open the diplomats discovered what is undoubtedly the largest dictator's den in the world. An obvious result of Adolf Hitler's two visits to Rome, his new office is patterned after Il Duce's princely diggings in the Palazzo Venezia, measures 88 by 47 ft to Mussolini's 60 by 40.

Like Il Duce's, the Führer's workshop is floored with highly polished marble, a red-brown stone taken from veins discovered while blasting for a new German highway. Like Il Duce's, Hitler's desk stands at the far end of the hall. On it last week were nine collared pencils, a case for the Führer's recent acquisition, eyeglasses, a large

Diplomats gathering in the Mosaiksaal *for the 1939 New Year reception. (© Ullstein: 00067674)*

In the Great Reception Hall, Hitler converses with the Japanese ambassador to Berlin during the 1939 New Year reception. (© Bildarchiv Preussischer Kulturbesitz)

magnifying glass, presumably for reading maps and blueprints, and several books: his own best-seller, *Mein Kampf*, Hans Frank's book of German law, directories of the Reichstag, Government offices and youth hostelries and – topmost – a volume on British and German battle lines during the World War. In another corner of the hall are a table, chairs and a sofa and, above them, a portrait of Bismarck. Elsewhere stands a bust of the late President Hindenburg, the man who admitted Hitler to the Chancellorship.

Five tall windows look out on a wide garden at the rear of the Chancellery. In the old Chancellery, it was the Führer's habit to leave his office every evening around 11 o'clock and walk in the rear garden for some time with his hands clasped behind his head. Then he would return, say to the guards on duty outside his door 'Goodnight, boys. Go to bed,' and continue working until about three. What he is working on has not been officially revealed but last week correspondents heard it was a sequel to *Mein Kampf*, the Nazi Bible.

The new work, as yet untitled, is expected to bear a relationship to the older book similar to that of the New Testament to the Old. In it Hitler reportedly will detail the fulfilment of many of the major prophecies of the old political testament, particularly the establishment of a Greater Germany through the Nazification of Austria and the Sudetenland. Germans will be informed that Germany's traditional hostility toward France has changed, not, however, because Germany has changed but because French policy toward Germany has been altered due to the fact that the French Government is now in the hands of war-scarred veterans who understand Germany better.

(* The German press announced last week that another new building, an enlarged Reichstag big enough to accommodate the deputies of an enlarged Germany, will soon be built on the site of the old legislative hall, which was gutted by the famous fire in 1933. German deputies, when they get together to shout approval of Adolf Hitler's desires, have been meeting since the fire in Berlin's Kroll Opera House.)

Two days after the New Year reception the entire corps of NSDAP Reichsleiters and Gauleiters were received; and on Monday 23 January, all bureaucrats and other personnel of the Chancellery staff took their places. By this time, however, rather more significant meetings had already taken place. On 18 January the professional chiefs of the three armed forces – Heer (Army), Kriegsmarine (Navy) and Luftwaffe (Air Force) – were invited to the Chancellery, soon to be followed by the entire general staff, the Kriegsakademie (War College), and German military attachés. The lesser gods of the Reich – more local and provincial leaders, directors of the German Post and Railways, and such lesser fry – had to wait; even intervention on their behalf by the Interior Minister could not convince Hitler of

During 1939 and 1940 the Chancellery hosted a series of diplomatic and other official gatherings for favoured guests. Once the war had started, however, the Chancellery was gradually emptied of its most valuable furniture and art, which were stored in the air raid shelters underground. (© Ullstein: 000166610)

the need to invite them. He was preoccupied by his old obsession with *Lebensraum*.

Hitler's eyes now turned back towards Czechoslovakia; the first experimental victim of the oppressive architecture of the New Reichs Chancellery would be the Czech President, Dr Emil Hácha.

In March 1938, Hitler had already pressured Austria into unification with Germany, making his triumphant entry into Vienna on 14 March. He next created a crisis over the German-speaking Sudetenland, a former German territory now part of Czechoslovakia. Hitler faced down Britain and France to obtain the Munich Agreement of September 1938, dismembering Czechoslovkia and returning the Sudetenland to Germany. Now he wanted more.

On 13 March 1939, Hitler put pressure on a former Catholic priest and Slovakian politician, Jozef Tiso, to declare Slovakian independence the next day.[63] Tiso had been just one among a coming and going of diplomats and advisers through the portals of the Chancellery during the preceeding weeks; some came from Budapest and Warsaw – following Munich, everyone wanted a piece of Czech territory. The second week of March had started with inflammatory German newspaper articles reporting from Prague that *'German boys are mishandled with brass knuckles . . . while Jews applaud . . . German houses are fired on by Czech armoured cars . . . Murder and arson rule again in the Czecho-Slovak Republic . . .'*, while German radio spread tales of *'Communists in Czech gendarmerie uniforms.'*

On Tuesday 14 March, at 4pm in the afternoon, Hitler summoned President Hácha to Berlin immediately for an urgent conference. Accompanied by his daughter and Foreign Minister Frantisek Chvalkovsky, Hácha boarded a special train, but this was delayed by congestion caused by German troop trains already on their way to Bohemia, and Hácha arrived in Berlin an hour late, at 10.40pm. The Czech diplomatic party were received with apparent consideration; the president's daughter was given a huge bouquet of yellow roses tied with a red bow on which was stamped a swastika. When they were

taken to the Adlon Hotel to wash up, they not only found their rooms filled with flowers, but also more steel-helmeted military sentries than usual – President Hácha was even invited to review some troops while he waited for the Führer's call. Hitler was in no hurry, and made the frail, elderly president wait – until 1am on Wednesday morning, when the summons to the Chancellery arrived at last.

Hácha was driven into the Ehrenhof and climbed the steps, entering the Anteroom. He was led across the awesome, echoing emptiness of the Mosaic Hall between its glowering cliffs of dark red-brown marble. At the far end he found himself in the dim, disorienting space under the dome of the Round Vestibule; everything about this chamber – the guidelines on the floor, its high circular construction – had been created by Speer to create the desired sense of tension and compression necessary for the *coup de théâtre* to follow. For on leaving the dark, claustrophobic

Reichsführer-SS Heinrich Himmler presents SS-Junkers (graduates of the SS leadership school at Bad Tolz) to Hitler in the Mosaiksaal. *(© Ullstein: 00022971)*

The Czech President Hácha is received in Hitler's study in he early hours of 15 March 1939. When he left the Chancellery later that day, his country had ceased to exist. (© Bundersarchiv: 146-1970-050-07)

drum, Hácha entered the seemingly endless Marble Gallery, a space whose extraordinary dimensions conspired to create an almost sublime impression of immeasurability and thus confusion. At the halfway point on the right-hand side the old gentleman was ushered through the doors beneath the great bronze shield embossed with the Führer's initials, between the two black-uniformed SS guards, and into the place where Czechoslovakia would meet its doom.

There he found not only Hitler and his aides, but numerous Army generals, who throughout the interview were periodically sent out for mysterious phone conversations with Prague. The aged President of Czechoslovakia was bullied into placing the fate of his countrymen in Hitler's hands. As Hitler reported it, 'At last I had so belaboured the old man that his nerves gave way completely, and he was on the point of signing.

Then he had a heart attack. In the adjoining room Dr Morrell gave him an injection, but in this case it was too effective. Hácha regained too much of his strength, revived, and was no longer prepared to sign, until I finally wore him down again.'

At 4.15am, President Hácha, still in conference, was handed a communiqué describing the conference and told to sign it; exhausted, he agreed. *'Both sides',* it read, *'unanimously expressed the conviction that the aim must be to assure calm, order and peace in this part of Central Europe. The Czechoslovak State President . . . trustfully laid the fate of the Czech people and country into the hands of the Führer of the German Reich. . .'.*

The late winter morning of 15 March 1939 was dawning when Emil Hácha at last left Speer's New Chancellery. Thirty minutes later, Hitler left for Anhalt station where he took the train to

Reichenberg in the Sudetenland. The next day, the German Army marched into Prague. Hitler considered that day as 'the most beautiful in his life', and he was convinced he would go down as 'The greatest German in history'. Czechoslovakia was divided. Hitler proclaimed, from Prague Castle, that Bohemia and Moravia were to become a German-controlled 'Protectorate'; what was left would be a small Slovak puppet state, while much of Slovakia and all of Subcarpathian Ruthenia were handed over to his ally Hungary.

Berlin, 20 April 1939

Church bells rang from swastika-decorated churches as the day began. The Chancellery had been transformed into a sea of flowers, palms and exotic plants. Servants in ceremonial uniforms with campaign medals on their chests stood

20 April 1939: Rudolf Hess, the Deputy Führer, presents Hitler with a 50th birthday gift in the Mosaiksaal.
(© Ullstein: 00734750)

waiting, or scurried from one room to another. Berlin and the German Reich were in a festive mood. The previous day Propaganda Minister Goebbels had made a special radio broadcast:

> In an unsettled and confused world, Germany tomorrow celebrates a national holiday in the truest sense of the word. It is a holiday for the entire nation. The German people celebrate the day entirely as a matter of the heart, not of the understanding.
>
> Tomorrow the Führer completes his fiftieth year. The entire German nation takes pride in this day, a pride in which those peoples who are friendly with us also take deep and hearty part. Even those who are neutral or oppose us cannot ignore the strong impact of the event. Adolf Hitler's name is a political programme for the entire world. He is almost a legend. His name is a dividing line. No one on earth can remain indifferent to his name. For some, he represents hope, faith, and the future, for others he is a target for confused hatred, base lies, and cowardly slander.
>
> The highest that a person can achieve is to give his name to an historical era, to stamp his personality indelibly on his age. Certainly the Führer has done that. One cannot imagine today's world without him . . .

That morning, Hitler's valet Linge woke him at 8am. Dressing himself in his brown Party jacket and dark trousers, Hitler replaced his usual brown leather 'Sam Browne' with the gold-laced belt of Commander-in-Chief of the Armed Forces.

In the Great Reception Hall his adjutant, Brückner, congratulated him in the name of the entire staff. Lined up behind stood his adjutants, liaison officers, bodyguard, his pilot Hans Baur with his flight team, and members of the Leibstandarte-SS in their black uniforms set off by scarlet Party armbands and white leather belt equipment. A military band struck up in the Ehrenhof.

The representatives of nations that he had already cowed paid him humble homage, while envoys from concerned neighbouring states rendered respectful tribute. Albert Forster of the Free City of Danzig, a frequent visitor to the

20 April 1939: Reichsmarschall Hermann Göring, on behalf of the State Cabinet, offers Hitler birthday congratulations in the Great Reception Hall. (© Bundesarchiv: 183-1988-0202-503)

Chancellery, presented him with a document declaring the Führer an honorary citizen of Danzig. Special delegations from Germany's allies were received in private audience. Meanwhile, all diplomats of 'friendly' nations, including the US chargé d'affaires, signed the birthday register at the New Chancellery. His Majesty King George VI of Great Britain sent the Führer the birthday greetings he customarily sent to all heads of state; however, the President of the United States – who usually congratulated only reigning monarchs on their birthdays – sent none, since the Führer had not answered the president's request for ten years' peace. Hitler owed President Roosevelt a letter.

The Reich's Cabinet ministers swore anew their 'faith in the word of Adolf Hitler', while Nazi Party leaders gathered in the Sports Palace to renew their oaths of loyalty. The 16th Bavarian Reserve Infantry Regiment, in which Corporal Hitler once served, issued a photographic album of the regiment's Great War history. From Propaganda Minister Goebbels came a symposium of German movies from 1910 to 1939. Labour Front Leader Dr Robert Ley presented a Volkswagen, the cheap mass-produced car that was not yet available to the Volk. On behalf of the Reichsbank Dr Walther Funk gave a version of Titian's 'Venus at the Mirror' (which official Germany now accepts as one of two authentic originals of this painting).

The common people were represented too; three rooms and part of the main Chancellery hall were piled high with birthday gifts. Peasants had sent examples of their regional handiwork; Westphalian women knitted 6,000 pairs of socks for the Führer's soldiers, and housewives got together to bake a 6-foot cake. From the more military-minded came pistols, hand grenades, an assortment of knives and daggers, and a live eagle (which the Führer would release in the Bavarian mountains). From the captains of industry he received models of tanks, aircraft, battleships and cannon.

But the real demonstration came on the streets of Berlin. Joined by the chiefs-of-staff, ministers and Party officials, the Führer left the Chancellery for a grand military parade.

In the Ehrenhof, the 1st Battalion of the Berlin garrison did the honours while a band played *'Deutschland, Deutschland über alles'* and the *'Horst-Wessel-Lied'*, the National Socialist anthem. As the Führer drove from the Chancellery to the Lustgarten on his way to review his birthday parade he was greeted by deafening storms of *'Heils!'*. On the new broad East-West axial road, which Hitler himself had ordered cut through the heart of a fast-rebuilding capital, the ruler of Germany showed the world the power of the Nazi regime. Above him flew 162 warplanes in formation. Before him passed in review – for four hours – the flower of his Army, some 40,000 men in full fighting equipment; between the field-grey blocks drove the most impressive war machines that Nazi Germany could muster: tanks, armoured cars, towed artillery. Interested foreign military attachés saw little that was new, but the representatives of small, trembling states could scarcely fail to be impressed.

The parade was followed by a state banquet in the Chancellery. Ministers, Reichsleiters, Gauleiters, SA and SS leaders, Wehrmacht chiefs-of-staff – everyone who had something to say in political or military Germany was present.

The next day, Hitler left for his mountain-top in the Obersalzberg.

On 19 April, Hitler had already received the members of the 'Blood Order' in the Mosaiksaal.[64] On 22 May, in the Great Reception Hall, Germany and Italy signed a formal alliance, the

19 April 1939: Hitler receives members of the 'Blood Order' in the Mosaic Hall. Award of this decoration marked injuries or imprisonment on behalf of the Nazi Party, between the abortive Munich putsch of November 1923 and Hitler's coming to power on 30 January 1933. (© Ullstein: 00042099)

so-called Pact of Steel; and on 7 June, in the Mosaiksaal, Hitler honoured the members of the German Condor Legion which had helped General Franco win the Spanish Civil War.

The years of victory, 1939–41

From the moment the Nazi Party came to power, Hitler sought to reverse the Treaty of Versailles by reuniting lost German-speaking territories with the new Reich. One of these was the predominantly German-speaking Free City of Danzig (Gdansk), which had been handed over to the new republic of Poland. In 1938 the German government increased its demands over Danzig, proposing that a highway be built to link Germany with East Prussia, thus cutting across the Polish territory of the Danzig Corridor leading north to Danzig on the Baltic coast. Afraid to become increasingly subject to the will of Germany, Poland rejected this proposal. Hitler made an

appeal to nationalism and promised to liberate German minorities in the Corridor as well as Danzig itself. A series of ultimata in pursuit of these claims, on Danzig and Memel, were the pretext for his declaration of war on Poland on 1 September 1939, thus unleashing World War II when, on 3 September, both Britain and France responded by declaring war on Germany. Poland was crushed in a matter of weeks; from 17 September the Soviet dictator Joseph Stalin colluded with Hitler, sending Red Army troops across his border to occupy eastern Poland.

After the fall of Poland came the period known as the 'Phoney War' when, during the winter of 1939–40, French and British armies faced the Wehrmacht across a static front line. Phoney or not, the war had been undertaken in a gamble that Germany could solve her near-bankruptcy by looting defeated nations. Her economy was totally inadequate to sustain a long war, and even

22 May 1939: Germany and Italy sign the 'Pact of Steel' in the Great Reception Hall. Here Hitler hands a copy of the treaty to his co-signatory, Mussolini's Foreign Minister Count Galeazzo Ciano. (© Bildarchiv Preussischer Kulturbesitz)

18 October 1939: Kapitänleutnant Günther Prien (standing beside Hitler) presents members of the crew of his U-47, during a reception at the Chancellery when they were decorated for the sinking of the British battleship HMS Royal Oak *inside the Scapa Flow anchorage a few nights previously. Prien, one of the first military 'stars' publicized by the wartime Propaganda Ministry, received the Iron Cross 1st Class and the Knight's Cross simultaneously on this occasion (the latter was only awarded to those who already held the former); his crew all received Iron Crosses. The commander-in-chief of the Kriegsmarine, Grossadmiral Erich Raeder, is at far left. Judging from the carpet pattern, this photo was taken in the Führer's Study.*
(© Bildarchiv Preussischer Kulturbesitz)

before the invasion of Poland, on 27 August 1939, strict rationing of all foodstuffs and other strategic materials had been imposed. In February 1940, Hermann Göring, as Plenipotentiary of the Four-Year Plan for German rearmament, ordered all metals useful for war production to be handed in or collected, and this had an impact even on the Reichs Chancellery.

On 13 March, the architect Carl Piepenburg wrote to Dr Lammers, informing him that all bronze fittings and even the railings of the staircases in the Old and New Chancelleries would be replaced with wood. In the meantime, construction work to finish and improve the building con-

tinued; on 29 March the architect informed Lammers that this work would last for another three to six months. By the end of March, Hitler had summoned the heads of the armed forces to the Chancellery to discuss his next gamble – the invasion of Denmark and Norway, in part to secure continuing iron ore supplies from Sweden through Norwegian coastal waters.

On 9 April 1940 the Germans struck north, achieving rapid success in little Denmark; but though the Allies were unready, a scratch force of British, French and Free Polish troops was landed in Norway, and inflicted significant casualties (particularly to the Kriegsmarine) before finally being expelled. This new war did not deter Hitler from paying attention to some improvements to his Chancellery, however. He asked for rest rooms for the chauffeurs of visitors and for his SS security men, while in the Old Chancellery he ordered new quarters and offices for his adjutants. The Ehrenhof and the Mosaiksaal were now finished; the air conditioning was replaced, and weather damage to the roof due to the severe winter was repaired. The space for SA archives was improved; Baldur von Schirach, head of the Hitler Youth, was given offices in the Chancellery, as was the commander of the Leibstandarte-SS, 'Sepp' Dietrich, and by mid 1940 all these alterations were complete.

On 10 May 1940, Hitler finally launched his armies in the greatest gamble yet: the invasion of the Low Countries and France. (That same day, the British formed a coalition government under Prime Minister Winston Churchill.) The new mobile warfare doctrine implemented by the German generals was stunningly successful; at the end of May the quarter-million men of the British Expeditionary Force had to retreat across the Channel, with great losses of equipment, aircraft and ships. On 10 June, Benito Mussolini (now sure which side would win) felt safe enough to bring Italy into the war as Germany's ally. On 22 June, France was forced to sign an armistice, giving up more than half the country to German occupation; from now on the collaborationist Vichy regime under Marshal Pétain would govern the southern half as friendly neutrals. In less than two months Germany had achieved the victory that had eluded her throughout World War I, occupying western, northern and central Europe from the Atlantic to the Soviet border in Poland, and with Italy, Hungary and Romania as subservient allies.

On the very day that France surrendered, Hitler summoned Speer and ordered him to resume planning and building for his new capital 'Germania' with the utmost urgency. On 6 July it was time to celebrate his greatest triumph; the victorious Führer arrived in his special train at Berlin's Anhalt station, to be welcomed by Göring, Hess, Goebbels, the Army chief-of-staff

Gen von Brauchitsch and Admiral Raeder. They drove to the Chancellery in a procession of gleaming black Mercedes, through streets thronged with crowds cheering and throwing flowers to the man who had at last wiped out the bitter memory of 1918. From Speer's balcony overlooking Wilhelmstraße, Hitler and his entourage reviewed a magnificent parade of victorious regiments returned from France. It was perhaps the most triumphant day of Hitler's life – certainly, it would never be equalled in the future.

The victors could not get enough of parades and festivities. On 19 July, during a speech at the Reichstag, Hitler announced the promotion to field marshal of Army chief-of-staff (OKH) Walther von Brauchitsch; the chief of the Joint Services staff (OKW), Wilhelm Keitel; three army group commanders – Gerd von Rundstedt, Wilhelm Ritter von Leeb, and Fedor von Bock; and four army commanders – Wilhelm List, Erwin von Witzleben, Walther von Reichenau and Günther von Kluge.[65] For the Luftwaffe, Generals Albert Kesselring, Erhard Milch and Hugo Sperrle were also raised to the marshalate. At 2pm on 14 August the newly promoted marshals of the Army were invited to the New Chancellery, where their marshals' full dress and undress batons were lying on the large marble-topped table in Hitler's study (the Luftwaffe marshals had to wait until 4 September before they could collect theirs).

Britain now stood alone against Germany. The U-boats and Luftwaffe began the Battle of the Atlantic, intended to cut off her lifelines for food and other vital supplies, and the tonnage of British shipping sunk rose alarmingly. The government led by Churchill rejected Hitler's overtures for a negotiated peace, and the Führer ordered bombing raids on the British Isles.

The Battle of Britain was the necessary prelude to the planned Operation 'Sealion', an amphibious and airborne invasion of the United Kingdom. As yet, London itself was a forbidden target, while Göring's squadrons concentrated on the Royal Air Force bases and radar stations that protected south-east England. The Luftwaffe failed in its attempt to gain air superiority for the

6 July 1940: Triumph. After driving in procession from the Anhalt Station, Hitler and his generals gather on the balcony overlooking Wilhelmstraße to review the parade to celebrate victory in the West. From left to right: Göring, Hitler, Admiral Raeder, Army chief-of-staff General Walther von Brauchitsch, Foreign Minister Joachim von Ribbentrop, and Joint Services Chief-of-Staff General Wilhelm Keitel. (© Ullstein: 00042647)

4 September 1940: The recently promoted field marshals of the Luftwaffe pose with Hitler after receiving their batons in his study. Flanking Hitler and Göring are (left) Erhard Milch and Hugo Sperrle, (right) Albert Kesselring. Just two days later Göring would make the fatal mistake of switching Luftwaffe attacks from British airfields and aircraft factories to London itself, thereby ensuring the RAF's victory in the Battle of Britain. (© Ullstein: 00734577)

invasion; and on the night of 24/25 August 1940 several German aircraft dropped their bombs on London in error.

Churchill had already stated that if London was bombed he would return the compliment the next day; this was simply a brave boast to keep up morale, considering the RAF's utter lack of readiness for strategic bombing in 1940. Nevertheless, it would prove to be the start of a murderous and devastating war from the air. To keep his promise and to show that Britain, undefeated, was able to strike blows deep inside the German Reich, the RAF organized its first air raid on Berlin on the night of 25/26 August 1940. The range of some 600 miles was extreme for the aircraft then available, and they could only bomb on clear summer nights. Fifty bombers took off on this very risky mission; they inflicted only token damage, mainly in the Berlin suburbs, and no casualties were recorded. During September, 15 more small raids followed. While the Luftwaffe inflicted ruinous damage and tens of thousands of casualties on British cities throughout the 'Blitz' of September 1940–May 1941, the RAF's navigation and bomb-aiming technology did not yet allow an effective response in hitting important targets.

Nevertheless, this was the first time in its history that Berlin (unlike London) had been bombed. As a precaution all windows in the Chancellery were protected by blinds against flying glass. Tapestries, carpets, paintings and statues were packed and taken into the air raid shelters under the New Chancellery.

A secret order of 9 September 1940 ordered the installation of a flak (anti-aircraft gun) battery on the Chancellery roof; it was initially manned by members of the Leibstandarte-SS, later replaced by soldiers from 1st Flak Division. (Early in 1942 the division stationed a stronger flak battery on the roof of the New Chancellery. As the unit comprised 154 officers and men the maintenance of security regulations became almost impossible, since they all needed access via Voss-Straße No.2. It was therefore decided that only the actual duty gun crews would remain in the building, and the unit headquarters and the rest of the battery were

given new quarters close by.)

Air raid shelters existed in Berlin, but only in small numbers. Before the war Hitler had ordered an extensive system of public shelters, but by the time war broke out only a handful of the 2,000 ordered were ready. By 1941, five huge public shelters were located in flak-towers (Flakturm). These enormous concrete towers had the dual function of providing shelter for citizens and also platforms for searchlights and AA guns. There were five of them, located at the Anhalt station, Kleistpark, the Zoo (Tiergarten), Friedrichshain and Humboldhain, with a total shelter capacity for 65,000 civilians. Other Berliners had to find refuge in the many U-Bahn stations and tunnels, or in their own cellars.[66] Further shelters were, of course, built under government buildings such as Göring's Air Ministry.

Meanwhile, affairs of state continued uninterrupted. A report in *Time Magazine:*

The morning of 27 September 1940 AD, which corresponds to the 18th year of the Fascist Era and the 15th year of *Showa,* dawned clear and quiet in Berlin.[67] There had been no air raid the night before and His Excellency Señor Don Ramón Serrano Suñer, Spain's Minister of Government and Falangist Party Leader, had had a good night's sleep. Don Ramón, who had been a visitor in Berlin for nearly three weeks, had, as usual, very little to do. He took a stroll in the direction of the Chancellery and on the way he ran into a phalanx of plum-cheeked school children, each carrying three paper flags – German, Italian and Japanese. They were on their way to the Chancellery to welcome Italy's Foreign Minister, Count Galeazzo Ciano.[68]

Don Ramón was not surprised to see the flags the children carried, but newspaper correspondents were. For a fortnight they had been led to expect that the big Axis doings which were obviously under way had to do with Don Ramón's country. While German Foreign Minister Joachim von Ribbentrop conferred with Count Ciano and Benito Mussolini in Rome they had filed Foreign Office-inspired dispatches about Axis designs on Gibraltar, on the Near East, on

Africa – but hardly a line about the Far East. This morning they learned that they had been thoroughly hoaxed. Lean, hollow-eyed Don Ramón had been posted in Berlin as a scarecrow to keep them out of the Axis chicken yard until another batch of eggs had hatched.

When the correspondents were admitted to the vast Hall of Ambassadors [sic] in the Chancellery, they observed that Don Ramón Serrano Suñer was not there. Neither was any member of the diplomatic corps except slim, suave Saburo Kurusu, who represents Japan in Berlin and has a Nazi-phobe American wife. Just outside a door that leads to the offices of Adolf Hitler a long table had been placed. Ambassador Kurusu sat there, as did Count Ciano and Herr von Ribbentrop. Before them, on the table, lay a thin document in triplicate.

At precisely 1.15 o'clock in the afternoon Foreign Minister von Ribbentrop scrawled his signature at the bottom of the first copy of the document, and addressed himself to duplicate and triplicate. Count Ciano followed him and Ambassador Kurusu signed last. The signing took two minutes. As Ambassador Kurusu laid down his pen the door behind him opened. With a nervous, catlike walk Adolf Hitler came in. He shook hands with the Italian and Japanese emissaries, sat down next to Ciano. Joachim von Ribbentrop stood up and through a battery of microphones proceeded to tell the world that Japan had joined the Axis.

On 5 December 1940, a carefully selected group of generals were invited by Hitler for a game in the reception hall of the Old Chancellery – a serious wargame, known by the Germans as *Kriegspiel*, which had been a planning tool of the general staff since the 19th century. Their opponent in these paper battles was the army of a state with which Hitler had signed a non-aggression pact on 23 August 1939: the Soviet Union. Four months after the wargame, on 30 March 1941, Hitler declared in the Chancellery that his forthcoming climactic contest againt the USSR would be a war of total destruction. The German People needed *Lebensraum,* and the vast expanses to the east would provide as much *raum* as they could wish.

March 1939: At centre, Prince Franz Josef II of Lichtenstein (who reigned from 1938 until his death in 1989), during an official visit to Hitler. After the German-Austrian Anschluss *of March 1938, the prince used his powers to force the formation of a coalition government in his miniature state, and – like Switzerland – Lichtenstein managed to stay neutral throughout World War II. He recalled of their meeting at the Chancellery in March 1939 that Hitler was 'visibly ill at ease', and did not make any impression on him at all during 90 minutes of smalltalk.*
(© Ullstein: 00807229)

The present inhabitants were not important; these sub-human Slavs would work as slaves, their commissars would be shot without mercy, and as for the Jews . . .

The implementation of Operation 'Barbarossa' could not be ordered at once, however, since the fumbling campaigns of his Italian ally in North Africa and the Balkans had to be rescued first. Hitler had already ordered the creation of a small but highly mobile Deutsches Afrika Korps, which arrived in Libya in February 1941 under the command of a junior but favoured general,

Erwin Rommel; at a time when British troops were being withdrawn to support Greece, Rommel rapidly took back much of the land from which the Italians had so recently been expelled. In April the Germans launched an invasion of Yugoslavia, quickly followed by that of Greece, and in May their paratroops captured (at great loss) the island of Crete, while Göring's Stukas took a heavy toll of the British Mediterranean Fleet.

At last free of these distraction, on 22 June 1941, at 10am Berlin time, 3 million German troops crossed the Soviet border in what was the greatest land operation ever seen up to that time. The previous night Hitler had dictated at the Chancellery his speech for the Reichstag, his secretaries Schroeder and Daranowski working in shifts in his study until 5am; the typed pages were immediately copied in the adjutants' room.

Twenty-two months after first invading Poland, Germany was fighting a war on two fronts, one of them against a nation whose almost limitless size had prevented its successful invasion since the Mongols swept across it from the east in the 13th century. As long ago as December 1939, at a crucial conference of generals at the Chancellery, Keitel – a political appointment, of very limited talents – had been the only general who had maintained that a two-front war was inevitable, and that the Führer should immediately attack Russia. In 1941 he had submitted to Hitler two memoranda on Russian preparedness, and urged an attack before the Russians were ready. The Red Army was indeed unprepared; its command echelons had been weakened by Stalin's purges, its equipment and its fighting doctrine were out of date, and despite numerous intelligence warnings Stalin refused to recognize the danger of a German invasion. Nevertheless, this was a gamble out of all proportion to anything Hitler had risked before; the Wehrmacht was greatly outnumbered, and its vital logistics were quite inadequate for operations over the vast distances involved.

For the first six months of 'Barbarossa' the advances achieved were staggering; the armoured spearheads raced across the steppes, encircling literally millions of bewildered Red Army troops for defeat at leisure by the following masses of German infantry and artillery. By the last months of 1941 Germany and her allies controlled almost all of mainland Europe from the Atlantic to the outskirts of Leningrad and Moscow; apart from the stubborn, battered island across the English Channel the only countries where field-grey soldiers could not strut were neutral Switzerland, Sweden, Spain and Portugal (the latter two of which might still choose to become Axis allies), and the toy states of Liechtenstein, Andorra, Vatican City and Monaco. The invasion had seized huge territories, including the Baltic states, Belarus and the vast grain-lands of Ukraine.

Hitler's headquarters and the Chancellery also profited directly from the captured Soviet territories; the Reichskommissar for the Ukraine, Koch, sent lavish quantities of flour, sugar, butter, meat, bacon, eggs and poultry to Berlin for the Chancellery kitchens.

Hitler had left his Chancellery on 24 June and moved to his field headquarters, known as the *Wolfsschanze* (Wolf's Lair), near Rastenburg in East Prussia. With some exceptions, such as his frequent trips to his home in the Obersalzberg, he would remain there for the next three years. Hans Heinrich Lammers took over the daily business of government, and only went to Rastenburg when he needed Hitler's advice or signature. (But even a man as well entrenched and useful as Lammers was not invulnerable to the jealousy of the rival Nazi leaders who jostled each other to capture the Führer's ear. In the second half of the war the power-conspirator *par excellence,* Martin Bormann, increasingly kept Lammers at a distance from the Führer, and by January 1945 the Chief of the Reich Chancellery was complaining that he had virtually lost his access to Hitler.)

In December 1941 the over-stretched and under-supplied Wehrmacht finally stalled before the gates of Moscow – thanks to the overconfidence of the Führer and some of his generals, the talents of Stalin's greatest soldier Georgi Zhukov, and the limitless capacity for endurance shown by the Russian people. Hitler blamed the generals, and dismissed Field Marshal von Brauchitsch;

from now on he would effectively act as his own Army chief-of-staff (a role for which he was abysmally unqualified).

Far away in hungry Britain, time had not stood still. So far in this war she had still lost more civilians than servicemen killed by enemy action, and as yet there was only one way she could retaliate. On 7 November 1941, Sir Richard Peirse, head of RAF Bomber Command, had launched a raid by more than 160 bombers on Berlin. More than 20 were shot down or crashed, while little or no damage was done to the military or economic installations in and around the capital. In February 1942 Sir Arthur Harris (later better known as 'Bomber' Harris) replaced Peirse, and German cities would soon experience the consequences of this change in command.

The slow turn of the tide, 1942–43

On 11 December 1941, four days after Japan's attack on Pearl Harbour, Germany declared war on the United States. Until now American shipping had only been vulnerable once it was on the high seas, taking part in the Atlantic convoys that brought vital provisions and war material to Britain. Now the U-boats could extend their operations into the coastal waters of the USA itself, and at first they achieved many sinkings. However, this success was nothing when weighed in the balance against the eventually catastrophic consequences for Germany. Hitler was now at war with the world's most widespread empire (Britain); the world's largest army (that of the Soviet Union); and the world's greatest industrial and financial power (the United States). Within a year, war production in the USA would overtake that of Germany, and it would never stop multiplying.

At around the same time, new four-engined bombers with longer range and much increased bomb-loads were coming into service with the RAF, in particular the Handley Page Halifax and the Avro Lancaster. However, during most of 1942 Bomber Command gave priority to attacking Germany's U-boat ports as part of Britain's effort to win the Battle of the Atlantic. During that whole year there were only nine air raid alerts in the German capital, none of them resulting in serious damage.

9 June 1942: The days of triumph are trickling away like sand in an hourglass. In the Mosaiksaal, *Hitler salutes the coffin of SS General Reinhard Heydrich, the State Protector of Bohemia-Moravia (i.e. the Führer's plenipotentiary in the occupied remnant of Czechoslovakia), who was mortally wounded in Prague on 29 May by Czech patriots parachuted from England. (© Ullstein: 00087594)*

On 4 November 1942, in the Western Desert of Egypt, the over-extended Italo-German forces of Field Marshal Rommel were routed by General Bernard Montgomery's British 8th Army in the second battle of El Alamein. This defeat finally denied Hitler any hope of seizing the Suez Canal and the Middle Eastern oilfields, and by May 1943 Axis forces in North Africa would be destroyed by combined British and US armies. On the Eastern Front the situation during that winter was even more disastrous.

An ambitious summer thrust as far as the Caucasus had failed to secure the Caspian oilfields, and Hitler had become mesmerized by the German 6th Army's struggle to capture the city of Stalingrad on the Volga. On 19 November, General Zhukov unleashed his brilliant Operation 'Uranus' north and south of that city, and on 22 November 6th Army was encircled. Hitler refused to allow any break-out; an attempted relief by Field Marshal von Manstein failed; the stupidity of Göring's boast that he could supply the enclave by air was soon revealed; and in February 1943 German resistance at Stalingrad ceased. These defeats in Africa and Russia cost Germany some half-a-million men, and she would never recover from them.

By this point most of Hitler's rare returns from Rastenburg to Berlin were in order to preside over state funerals. On 16 December 1941 he attended that of Hans Kerrl (a completely powerless Reichsminister of Church Affairs); on 12 February 1942 came the obsequies for Fritz Todt (the engineer and Reichsminister for Armaments and Munitions, killed in a plane crash). On 9 June 1942 Hitler participated in the last rites for a colleague much more intimately involved in the Nazi hierarchy – SS General Reinhard Heydrich, Chief of the Reich Main Security Office and Reichs Protector of Bohemia and Moravia, who was assassinated by Free Czech agents. All these funerals were held in the Chancellery, where the Mosaiksaal was transformed into a kind of Nazi state chapel, with tall brass candlesticks, banners, and open fires to the left and right of the bier.

It was to that hall that Goebbels summoned, on 15 February 1943, all the high-ranking Party officials, to be harangued about the need for 'total war' and reassured with promises of future victories and secret weapons. To regain the initiative on the Russian Front, in July Hitler ordered a massive new offensive on the Kursk salient in southern Ukraine. He committed the bulk of his remaining Panzer divisions, spearheaded by his most trusted Waffen-SS formations and battalions of the new Panther and Tiger tanks. After huge losses of men and equipment on both sides this Operation 'Citadel' failed, and during late 1943 the Wehrmacht slowly retreated across Ukraine towards the Soviet-Polish border. The Allies were now ashore in Italy and fighting Marshal Kesselring's occupying army, and Mussolini, a shadow of his former bombastic self, now ruled only a rump Fascist state in the north.

In the night skies over Germany itself, Sir Arthur Harris' Bomber Command was steadily increasing its strength and its sophistication. Night bomb-aiming was inherently too inaccurate for precision bombing of high-value military and industrial targets; Harris pursued for the carpet-bombing of both the industrial and the residential areas of whole cities, to damage German war production and also to break civilian morale, while the US 8th Army Air Force – now based in England – would fly precision raids by daylight. On the night of 5 March 1943 the first of a number of new radio-location devices were carried by fast Mosquito aircraft, followed immediately by highly trained 'Pathfinders' to drop coloured markers; these enabled a raid on Essen by more than 400 bombers to achieve better results than before. This 'Battle of the Ruhr' over the western industrial cities continued until summer, with an average of 400 bombers inflicting unprecedented damage during 43 main raids (though at a heavy cost in RAF bombers and aircrew). It was followed at the end of July by the four raids of the 'Battle of Hamburg'; in conjunction with US daylight raids, Harris burned the heart out of this important harbour city, killing 42,000 people, injuring another 100,000 and destroying 225,000 homes and 3,600 businesses. While raids contin-

7 September 1943: Alfred Rosenberg, Minister for the Eastern Territories, reads a eulogy in the Mosaiksaal *over the coffin of the assassinated Wilhelm Kube, his State Commissioner at Minsk in Belarus. (© Ullstein: 00131569)*

ued on many cities, this concentrated success was not repeated that summer, but the public shock in Germany was immense. (Hitler never visited bombed areas, and it was Goebbels who showed himself to have the common touch.)

Although Germany's military and economic situation was deteriorating on all fronts, the creator of the Chancellery had risen to new heights. Albert Speer had been appointed to succeed Todt as Armaments Minister in 1942, and in 1943 his considerable talents for organization – and Hitler's continuing favour – brought him the overall direction of the war economy. Speer proved an inspired appointment; he made great strides in decentralizing industrial production, prefabrication techniques, and finding alternatives to scarce materials, and in 1944 production of some items would even be higher than it had been in 1940. His immediate adversaries in this struggle would be Air Vice Marshal 'Bomber' Harris by night, and his American counterpart General Carl Spaatz by day.

The first battle of Berlin: the air war 1943–45

Harris launched the 'Battle of Berlin' on the night of 18/19 November 1943. More than 800 heavy bombers flew on any given night, equipped with new and more sophisticated navigational aids. The formidable German night-fighter defences would be confused by alternating raids on the capital with attacks on other cities, and by diversionary missions flown by only a few fast Mosquitoes. However, between November 1943 and March 1944 Bomber Command made 16 massed attacks on Berlin.

The first raid on 18/19 November was by about 440 Lancasters guided by four Mosquitos; however, thick cloud limited the damage. A second raid on 22/23 November, by 469 Lancasters, 234 Halifaxes, 50 Stirlings and 11 Mosquitos (753 bombers) was the most effective yet, causing extensive damage to residential areas west of the centre – Tiergarten, Charlottenburg, Schöneberg and Spandau – and the dry weather led to several massive fires. Among the buildings destroyed were the Kaiser Wilhelm Memorial Church, the French, Italian and Japanese embassies, Charlottenburg Palace, the Berlin Zoo, the Ministry of Munitions, the Waffen-SS Administrative College, the barracks of the Imperial Guard at Spandau, and several arms factories.

These devastating raids caused heavy loss of life; that of 22nd/23rd killed 2,000 Berliners and rendered 175,000 homeless. The following night a raid by 383 bombers killed another 1,000 and made 100,000 homeless. On 24–26 November only feint raids were flown by Mosquitoes; then on 26th/27th another 443 bombers hit the capital, causing most damage in the semi-industrial suburb of Reinickendorf. The attacks continued at regular intervals:

2/3 December: 440 Lancasters and Halifaxes – mainly inaccurate and to the south of the city, but two Siemens factories, a ball-bearing factory and several railway installations were damaged.

16/17 December: 483 Lancasters – heavy damage to railway system; 1,000 wagon-loads of war material destined for the Eastern Front held up for nearly a week. National Theatre and military and political archives destroyed. By this time the cumulative effect of the bombing campaign had destroyed more than a one-quarter of Berlin's total living accommodation.

23/24 December: relatively light damage.

28/29 December: 709 heavy bombers, but only light damage.

1/2 January 1944: 421 Lancasters.

2/3 January: 371 Lancasters and Halifaxes. German night fighters did not intercept until the bombers were over Berlin, but shot down 27 Lancasters.

During December 1943 and January 1944 repeated raids killed several hundred people each night and rendered anything between 20,000–80,000 homeless each time; in all, nearly 4,000 Berliners were killed, 10,000 injured and 450,000 made homeless during those two months alone. The largest raid was on the night of 15/16 February 1944, when Harris sent 561 Lancasters and 314 Halifaxes to the capital. Despite cloud cover many important industrial targets were hit, including the large Siemensstadt area, with the central and south-western districts sustaining most damage.

The night bombing of Hitler's capital would continue until the end of March 1944, and from 6 March the USAAF – now benefiting from long-range escort fighters – also raided Berlin by day. In April the strategic bombing effort had to be switched to preparing for the Normandy landings. In all, between 18 November 1943 and 31

Damage to Voss-Straße and the Chancellery after a British air raid on the night of 29 January 1944. (© Bundesarchiv: 146-1983-028-04)

March 1944 the Allies flew about 20,200 sorties to Berlin; the price was nightly losses averaging about 5 per cent (which meant between 250 and 300 aircrew lost each night). In these three-and-a-half months Berlin suffered some 75,000 people killed, and up to 3 million made homeless. The one thing Harris did not achieve, however, was the breaking of the German spirit of resistance.

That the Allied bombs killed Germans without discrimination could be read in *Time Magazine* on Monday 8 May 1944:

The war had struck close to Hans Hube. His son had been killed on the Eastern front; his daughter had died in an air raid on Berlin. He himself, the Reich's famed one-armed tank general, had barely managed to slip out of the Russians' reach on the hostile Ukrainian steppe.

On Hitler's birthday, straight-backed Hans Hube journeyed to Berlin, stood at stiff attention while the Führer pinned Oak Leaves to [his] Ritterkreuz (Knight's Cross) . . . Germany needed heroes; the Nazi press obediently hailed the 53-year-old general.

A few hours later dark news was brought to Hitler: Colonel-General Hans Valentin Hube had died in an air accident. Last week at the Mosaic Hall of the Chancellery, Hitler, Göring, and smaller Nazi fry met to mourn the 32nd Nazi general officer lost in World War II.[69]

During the constant air raids most of the Chancellery and the 'Wilhelmstraße' or Government District had been spared, but damage became quite visible. On the corner of Voss-Straße and Hermann-Göring-Straße, just above the restaurant in the administration wing, a bomb had fallen through the roof. By late January 1944 most of the glass skylights and cupolas that brought daylight into the galleries and state rooms were destroyed, as well as the hanging lamps; all glass was removed and replaced with fibreboard. By now, most of the State Apartments had been emptied and everything was stored in the air raid shelters. It was only for special occasions, such as General Jodl's staff meeting on 5 May 1944, that some galleries were refurnished, and they were emptied again afterwards.

Already stretched on both the Mediterranean and Russian fronts, the Wehrmacht suffered two strategic disasters in the summer of 1944. On 6 June, Operation 'Overlord' put US, British and Canadian armies ashore on the coast of Normandy, and despite savage fighting they maintained and expanded their beachhead. By August, when the German armies in France collapsed and fell back towards the Low Countries and the Rhine, a vast stretch of the central Russian Front had also been forced backwards by the Soviet Operation 'Bagration'.[70]

Criticism of the government became more and more public. Many Germans were shocked by the bomb attempt on Hitler's life on 20 July 1944, but even the Führer – previously largely immune from the public cynicism about his Party underlings – was now fair game. As early as 28 February 1944 someone had scrawled in a storage room between

the entrance at Voss-Straße No.6 and the Marmorgalerie: *'Adolf Hitler, even you have to die.'* Given the strictly limited access to the building, this must have been the work of one of the Chancellery staff or guards.

With fighting on three fronts, dwindling oil supplies and constant Allied bombing, German-occupied territory was steadily being lost to Allied advances. As the Red Army neared East Prussia, German civilians would begin to flee westwards en masse from Prussia and Silesia, fearing the revenge of the Soviet soldiers. They began to hear atrocity stories – both true, and short-sighted propaganda from Goebbels' usually more intelligent ministry – and most Germans rightly believed that they would be safer under Western than Soviet occupation. As the Red Army approached from the east, the RAF carried out a series of attacks on cities in eastern Germany, swollen with refugees; spared until now, cities such as Dresden would suffer terribly from being transport hubs through which troops and materiel were passing on the way east to the fighting front. Nevertheless, Berlin still got its share of attention.

One of the most famous daylight raids was that of 3 February 1945, when almost 1,000 B-17 Flying Fortresses of the US 8th Army Air Force, protected by P-51 Mustangs, attacked the Berlin railway system in the belief that the 6th SS Panzer Army was moving through the capital by train on its way to the Eastern Front. The 3,000 tons of bombs dropped in one of the heaviest raids ever suffered by Berlin killed between 2,500 and 3,000 people and left some 120,000 homeless. The raid severely damaged the Berlin newspaper district of Kreuzberg, the central area, and some other areas such as Friedrichshain. Government and Nazi Party buildings were also hit, including the Reichs and Party Chancellery, the Gestapo headquarters, and the People's Court. The Unter den Linden, Wilhelmstraße and Friedrichstraße areas were turned into seas of ruins. One of the victims was none other than Roland Freisler, the infamous head of the People's Court, who was conducting a Saturday session when the Berlin air raid sirens sounded.[71]

For the first time, damage to the Chancellery

was severe, including to Hitler's private apartments in the Old Chancellery, where the entrance, dining room and conservatory were seriously hit. Water, electricity supply and the telephone connections were interrupted, and the heating system was knocked out for several days.

One day, the architect Hermann Giesler arrived at the Chancellery with the last part of the large scale model for Hitler's planned redevelopment of his home city of Linz as the future cultural capital of the Greater German Reich. It was taken down to the shelters and fitted into place. On 9 February, Hitler went to see it; for several hours he discussed with Giesler how the work would proceed once the war was over. It was probably the last time that Hitler was able to lose himself in dreams of being the 'Führer Master-Builder'.

On 24 February 1945, Hitler summoned the Party's Reichsleiters and regional Gauleiters to the Chancellery. Some of them were missing; Gauleiters Koch of East Prussia and Hanke of

Lower Silesia were both cut off from Berlin by the Soviet advances. All who did attend gave the stooped, shaking and prematurely-aged Führer a sympathetic reception. Germany was going to win the war; National Socialism was going to beat the Soviet Army in the suburbs of Berlin. Two days later, on 26 February, another big air raid destroyed the homes of some 80,000 citizens. Raids continued until April, when the Soviet Army was already outside the city, and in the last days of the war the Soviet Air Force joined in the efforts of the RAF and USAAF. By that time the capital's civil defences and infrastructure were on the point of collapse.

By the end of March 1945 the Western Allies were across the Rhine and racing across west Germany, but almost every man, boy, gun, tank and aircraft that the Wehrmacht had left was directed towards the east. Soviet forces were threatening the last lines of resistance both north-east and south-east of the capital.

During one of the air raids a bomb had blown a hole in the roof at the corner of Hermann-Göring-Straße (left) and Voss-Straße. Although it was repaired, this photo taken immediately after the end of the war shows damage at the same place. In the left background, above the edge of the deep shadow on the western face, the orangery at the north side of the garden can be seen still standing, although its tall windows have been blown out. (© Bildarchiv Preussischer Kulturbesitz)

10 Hitler's Last Headquarters

Air raids had been anticipated from the first rebuilding projects in Wilhelmstraße, and Hitler ordered the construction of an air raid shelter under the Old Chancellery when he commissioned Professor Gall to design the new reception hall in the Chancellery garden. The building of the new dance floor provided perfect cover for this confidential project, and during the construction work between July 1935 and January 1936 Firma Hochtief AG incorporated what became known as the *Vorbunker* beneath this. To give extra protection, the cellars of the Old Chancellery surrounded this bunker.

The entrance to the bunker was via the reception hall, close to the toilets and vestibule, where two doors provided Hitler with direct access close to his private apartments.

When Speer was ordered to build the New Chancellery his brief included a series of air raid shelters for the Chancellery staff. These consisted of a network of several main shelters, some smaller rooms, tunnels and emergency exits.[73] The whole consisted of some 70 rooms divided between two main complexes. The first comprised two massive garages with workshops, quarters for the drivers and a command office, situated under gardens behind the two guard barracks in Hermann-Göring-Straße; this was

A striking visual metaphor for Hitler's mood of denial as his time finally ran out: he studies the model for the redevelopment of his home city of Linz, Austria, completed in the Chancellery air raid shelters for his approval on 9 February 1945. (© Ullstein: 00444655)

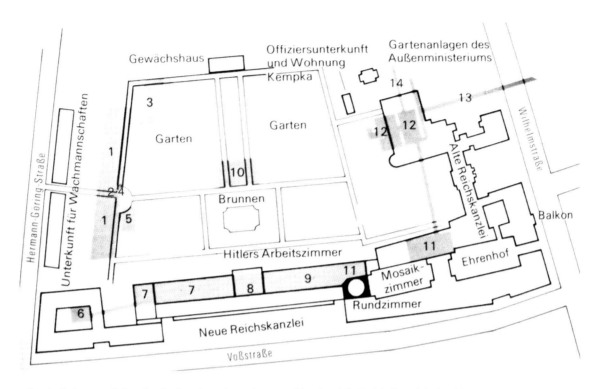

The shaded parts of this sketch plan show the underground levels of the Reichskanzlei. *(1, 1) Main underground garages. (2) Offices and quarters for drivers. (3) Workshops. (4) SS-Ostugaf Kempka's office. (5) Bunker for 50 drivers. (6) Small garage under West wing – a reported tunnel connecting this via the coal- and lorry-lift to the main garages at (1) is not shown here. (7, 7) Kitchens and washing facilities. (8) Hospital with operating theatre. (9) Air raid shelter for civilian staff. (10) Parking for ten cars – there is some pictorial evidence for this. (11, 11) Shelters for Hitler's staff and adjutants; the passage leading north to (12) was called the 'Kannenberggang'. (12, 12) The Haupt- or Führerbunker, left, and the Vorbunker, right. (13) Passage under Wilhelmstraße leading to Propaganda Ministry. (14) Passage leading up Wilhelmstraße to Foreign Office.*

the domain of Hitler's senior driver and commander of the motor pool, Erich Kempka, who was given the SS rank of Obersturmbannführer (SS-Ostubaf, lieutenant-colonel). The second was a series of six large subdivided chambers underneath the Central block or Mittelbau of the New Chancellery. Heavy steel doors separated the six large compartments, each of them subdivided into smaller rooms. Each main compartment had an emergency exit leading towards Voss-Straße; these led to and were sealed by heavy hydraulic doors in the pavement between the façade of the Mittelbau and the balustrade.

With the start of British air raids on Berlin, Hitler ordered the preparation of underground quarters for those who were indispensable to state affairs. In the shelters of the New Chancellery 53 rooms were reserved for ministerial personnel. Under the East wing at Voss-Straße Nos.2–4 were another 26 rooms, this compartment measuring 60m by 20m (197ft by 65ft 7in) and protected by a ceiling 1.70m (5ft 7in) thick.

Further shelters were planned; in the meantime, probably for reasons of propaganda, Hitler opened some of the existing bunkers under the New Chancellery to certain categories of the public. A total of 69 rooms, of which 50 were beneath the Mittelbau – under Hitler's study – were made accessible for pregnant women and children under the age of six years, and beds, heating and sanitary facilities were installed.[74]

Later, in mid-1943 when air raids became routine, more rooms were opened to Berliners.

When the siege of Berlin became imminent, Hitler ordered the organization in the underground shelters of a field hospital with a capacity of 500 to 700 beds for military and civilian use, under the direction of Professor Haase. Four other rooms, two at each side of the field hospital, were reserved for Hitler's aides and military and civilian staff. A kitchen-canteen was situated beneath the Great Reception Hall, where meals were served until almost the last days of the war. From this part of the bunker complex two tunnels led west and north; one connected the main chambers with a small underground garage for two staff cars and two armoured half-tracks, and the second with the main underground garages behind Hermann-Göring-Straße. The heavy-duty coal- and lorry-lift connected with the small garage, from which an exit also emerged directly onto the pavement of Herman-Göring-Straße, disguised so that passers-by would not notice it.

On the eastern side of the bunker complex, towards the Borsig Palace and the Old Chancellery, the outer room to the right was connected via a tunnel to another, smaller room situated near the entrances of the Anteroom and State Dining Room. From this underground room, equally reserved for Hitler's aides and military staff, ran the *'Kannenberggang'* leading north to the Vorbunker beneath the Old Chancellery reception hall – so-named after Artur Kannenberg, Hitler's butler, because he also used it for storage.

From the Vorbunker, tunnels led both north to the Foreign Ministry, and east to the Propaganda Ministry on the other side of Wilhelmstraße. In this underground complex were located the telephone exchange of Hitler's headquarters (*'Alt 500'*), the radio room, the press office, and – in the final days – the command post of SS Battle-Group Mohnke. About 60 to 70 SD men were also stationed there under the command of a Criminal Police officer, SS-Sturmbannführer Foster; these were responsible for security in the bunker, and searched everyone who went in or out.

With the development of heavier aerial bombs Hitler became increasingly anxious about the strength of the Vorbunker, which had a ceiling 1.6m (5ft 3in) thick. On 18 January 1943 he ordered Speer to build a second, deeper bunker with a ceiling 3.5m (11ft 6in) thick and walls of 3.5m-4m (up to 13ft), while the interior surfaces had to appear the same as in the old bunker. Again, Speer gave a contract to Firma Hochtief AG, and under the supervision of the architect Piepenburg work started on digging the necessary 10m (33ft) excavation, linked to the west side of the Vorbunker but on a deeper level. The Vorbunker would also receive an extra meter of concrete to reinforce its roof. The new *Hauptbunker* was connected to the old one by means of an

When the New Chancellery was built a heavy duty coal-lift was installed behind the West wing, with direct access to the storage cellars and to the underground garages behind the barrack blocks on Herman-Göring-Straße. During the last months of the war, generals used this lift when they arrived to attend the daily staff conferences.
(© Ullstein: 00067620)

airlock and angled stairs. Both were equipped with generators and all necessary supplies so as to be independent of one another. It would not be until 23 October 1944 that Dr Lammers could inform Hitler that the bunker was in all respects ready for use.

Entering the Vorbunker, one passed through an airlock to arrive in a small room, where one door opposite the entrance gave access to the passage leading towards the garden of the Foreign Ministry. On the left was another shielded door, which led into the Vorbunker with its 20 rooms. The first compartment one entered was a corridor-like space divided by a heavy steel door into two separate rooms, one 7m by 3.5m (19ft 7in by 11ft 6in) and the second 3.5m square. The longer section of the corridor was also used as a dining room by those quartered in the Vorbunker. Off the right of this corridor was the machinery and air-filter room, and to the left two small rooms with showers and toilets. Hitler's secretaries, members of the Führer-Begleitkommando and the policemen of the SD used other rooms in the Vorbunker (Frau Goebbels and her children would eventually occupy three more rooms on the other side of the guardroom).

Following the corridor, one entered an airlock that gave access to an angled staircase leading downwards towards the actual Führerbunker. The size of the new bunker was identical to the old one, with internal walls of 0.5m (1ft 8in) reinforced concrete.

From the angled staircase the visitor arrived in a large guardroom that gave access to the actual bunker. There, a corridor divided into equal near and far ends separated the bunker into left and right sides. From the first half of the corridor, the rooms on the left and right were machinery and air-filter rooms, telephone exchange and radio room, plus toilets and showers. Moving on into the second half of the corridor, one found on the right side quarters for orderlies, Hitler's' doctors, etc, and on the left were Hitler's and Eva Braun's rooms. Hitler's accommodation was furnished with chairs, tables, sofas, closets and paintings brought down from the Chancellery. The corridors, due to lack of space, were also used as dining and conference rooms.

The following extract from a Soviet interrogation report adds many domestic details to this basic description:

From the old bunker [Vorbunker] a connecting [shaft] to the new was broken through with a staircase, which ended in a small chamber with an armoured door. Behind this door began the broad, two-part passageway of the Führerbunker.

In the near half of the passageway stood, on the right wall, cabinets with air raid equipment (gas masks, fire-fighting equipment, etc). A door in this wall led to the machinery room and air-conditioning plant. The second armoured door led into six adjoining rooms. Here was a telephone station operated by an officer of Hitler's bodyguard, a telephone switchboard and a telegraph. [Others were] Dr Morell's room, a first-aid station – where there was also a bed for Dr Ludwig Stumpfegger, the emergency physician; a sleeping room for Heinz Linge and orderly officers; and a social room.

Against the left wall in the first half of the corridor stood a four-cornered table and an armchair. A wall clock hung over the table. Nearby was a telephone station, from which the watch sergeant of the telephone service announced trunk calls to the participants in the situation conferences. A door on the left side led to washrooms. There Hitler's Alsatian 'Blondi' had her place.[75]

An armoured door separated the first half of the corridor from the second, the reception room. At the entrance to the reception section stood an officer of the bodyguard. In the reception section, the participants assembled before the situation conferences and waited for Hitler. On the wall hung large paintings, mostly landscapes. Against the right wall stood 12 to 16 armchairs. On the opposite wall was a cushioned bench, in front of which stood a four-cornered table with cushioned chairs. To the right and left of the cushioned bench were two armoured doors. The left [-hand door] led into the rooms of Hitler and Eva Braun, the right into the situation conference room.

In front of Hitler's apartment was a little refreshment room. In front of its door stood a screen, which blocked the view into the rooms of Hitler and Eva Braun from those in the passage-way.

Behind the double door of the refreshment room was Hitler's office, laid with a thick, soft carpet. On the table was a bronze lamp, inkstand, telephone, world atlas, a magnifying glass and usually the Führer's spectacles. Over the table hung one of Menzel's paintings, a half-length portrait of Frederick II in an oval frame. Against the opposite wall stood a sofa, and in front of it there was a table and three coloured silk-covered chairs. A still life hung over the sofa. To the right of that stood a tea table, to the left a radio receiver. On the right wall hung a painting by Lucas Cranach.

A door in the same wall led to Hitler's bedroom, likewise carpeted. Here was a bed with a night table, a clothes cabinet, a mobile tea table on castors, and a safe in which he kept his secret papers, book shelves, and oxygen apparatus. To the left in Hitler's office was a door to Hitler's and Eva Braun's bathroom. From the bathroom a door led to Eva Braun's toilet and bedroom. Here stood at the right of the door a dark couch, a small round table and an armchair. Opposite the couch against the far wall stood Eva Braun's bed, a clothes cabinet, and a box for her dog. On the floor was a dark, fancy-flowered carpet. The walls were decorated with flower paintings. The second door from Eva Braun's room led into the refreshment room.

At the end of the reception section was the so-called 'airlock' with armoured door. In the airlock were the right and left emergency exits to the park behind the Chancellery. A winding stair-case led up [to] the right exit, [and to] the left, a steel staircase like a fireman's ladder. This exit was roofed with a dome-shaped tower with machine-gun ports, in which was an observation post. SS personnel from the bodyguard manned the watch in the tower. The tower had telephone communication with the Führerbunker.

The Führer returns

After the failure of the Ardennes offensive in December 1944–January 1945, Hitler and his staff left the Adlerhorst headquarters at Bad Nauheim on 15 January in great haste. Taking the Führer's special train from Giesen, they arrived the next day in Berlin. Hitler moved into his private apartment in the Old Chancellery, where his arrival was kept secret – his personal flag was not flown over the building.[76]

His immediate staff and servants returned to their rooms on the first floor of the right wing in the Old Chancellery. General Wilhelm Burgdorf (Hitler's military adjutant since October 1944) was the only newcomer. Kannenberg and his wife returned to their flat on the ground floor, close to the rooms of Linge, the cook and a female servant. Soon afterwards they would be joined by Eva Braun, who also took up residence in the Old Chancellery in the room next to Hitler's apart-ment.

On 30 January, the 12th anniversary of the Nazi regime, Hitler made his last radio broadcast.

In the middle of February, due to the increasing air raids, Hitler moved down into the Führerbunker. His immediate entourage and staff remained in the Old Chancellery, or looked for refuge in the labyrinth of shelters situated under the New Chancellery.

Twice a day Hitler had received situation reports, at first in the conservatory of the Old Chancellery and later, after its destruction by a bomb early in February, in his official study in the New Chancellery. The first conference took place at 3pm and the second at around midnight. After mid-February the Führer left the bunker only for these daily afternoon conferences and for lunch, which he took in the Old Chancellery; he ate dinner in the bunker, where the night conferences always took place.

When the regular participants in the afternoon briefings arrived they had to wait in the antechamber next to Hitler's study, where SS soldier-servants served alcoholic drinks and cold snacks. Hitler, accompanied by his valet Linge, arrived from the emergency exit of the bunker through the garden of the Chancellery, entering his study via the terrace and the French windows. Once inside, he directed Linge to ask the others to join them. The SS men of his bodyguard opened the doors to his office, where the situation maps were already spread out on Albert Speer's great marble-topped table.

Bernd Freytag von Loringhoven, *aide de camp* to the Army chief-of-staff General Guderian, remembered:

> The daily briefings were then held in the Führer's spacious office in the New Chancellery . . . In one corner of the office the participants gathered around an enormous marble console table used for spreading out the maps. Furniture, pictures and tapestries had been removed, [to be] sheltered from the bombing. In case of an air raid alarm – and this happened more frequently from February 1945 – the meetings were switched to the small conference room in the bunker.

On 12 January 1945, the Red Army started its great offensive to force what was left of the German armies in the East back into Germany, Czechoslovakia and Austria. In the northern sector this meant breaking the Wehrmacht's line along the River Vistula in Poland. In fierce fighting the Soviets began to create a huge salient pointing towards Berlin; resistance was often desperate but was soon overcome, and after advancing at the rate of up to 40km (25 miles) a day the first Soviet troops were crossing the Polish/German border by 20 January. By the 29th, General Zhukov had reached the last natural obstacle – the River Oder, only about 60km (40 miles) east of Berlin – and had seized limited bridgeheads, but lack of supplies then halted his advance. In mid-February a newly created German Army Group Vistula (nominally commanded by Reichsführer-SS Himmler, but actually by Generals Wenck and later Heinrici) attempted a counter-offensive down from Pomerania into the northern flank of the Soviet bulge; this failed, but it persuaded Zhukov to invest troops and time in clearing East Prussia and Pomerania.

During March, from the Baltic coast in the north all the way south down to Lake Balaton in Hungary, on an S-shaped front of about 1,400km (850 miles), six Soviet army groups were driving across East Prussia, Pomerania, Poland, Silesia, Czechoslovakia and Hungary into Germany and Austria. All of these thrusts tied down the dwindling and overstretched Wehrmacht; but the nearest Soviet armies, on the Oder due east of Berlin, hardly moved.

By the middle of March, Hitler – who no longer wished to leave the bunker at all – had changed the time of the daily situation conferences, all of which now took place underground. He would wake up only at between 1pm and 1.30pm, and the first meeting started at about 4pm and lasted until 6pm or 7pm. Due to the nightly air raids on Berlin, which made any movement in the city difficult or impossible before about midnight, the next meeting was held around 2am or 3am. Depending on the length of that night's raid, the nightly situation reports lasted for about an hour. After the conference Hitler would settle down to 'evening' tea in his study with Eva Braun and his secretaries Frau Christian and Frau Junge. Up in the smoking room of the Old Chancellery members of his entourage – such as General Burgdorf, SS General Fegelein and SS Major Günsche – would drink vodka and cognac, no doubt relieved to be able to smoke at will.

In this critical situation the greater part of Hitler's fleet of cars had already been sent to the Obersalzberg, and his special train was hidden in a wood near Munich. His personal flight, consisting of 15 four-engined Focke-Wulf Fw 200 Kondors and old Junkers Ju 52 trimotors, was sitting at the ready on Gatow airfield, 20km (12 miles) west of Berlin, in case they were needed to take the Führer and his entourage out of the capital at short notice.

The living conditions in the Führerbunker deteriorated steadily during its roughly three months of use. Berlin has a high water-table, and a cool moistness was noticeable in the rooms. Many witnesses later spoke of the constant droning sound of the ventilation system. This system, with its filters against poison gas attacks, was not perfect. During one of the situation conferences when generals packed into the bunker it was suddenly noticed that fumes were entering the conference room – everyone present jumped to the conclusion that this was another plot to kill Hitler and his entourage. The fresh-air intake ventilators were switched off and a search was started. After some time the cause was found: in the garage Göring's chauffeur had parked his car, running on a wood-gas generator, underneath the air intake duct, and had left its engine running to keep warm. From then on the space beneath the intake duct was sealed off to cars.

On 6 March, Hitler appointed General Helmuth Reymann, a veteran of the Eastern Front, as the commander of the Berlin Defence Area, replacing General Bruno Ritter von Hauenschild. On 20 March he appointed General Gotthard Heinrici to command Army Group Vistula; Himmler's nominal appointment had been a joke, and the competent General Wenck had been injured in a car crash. On 27 March, Dr Lammers, Hitler's Chief of Chancellery, saw him for the last time; he complained of high blood pressure, and Hitler sent him to Berchtesgaden on sick leave.

On 9 April the besieged East Prussian capital, Königsberg, finally fell to the Red Army, allowing Rokossovsky's 2nd Belarussian Front (army group) to move west. During the first two weeks of April the Red Army redeployed its forces for the final act. Zhukov concentrated his 1st Belarussian Front into the central sector, facing the Seelöwe Heights overlooking the west bank of the Oder. Rokossovsky's 2nd Belarussian Front moved into position to his north, while to his south Konev's 1st Ukrainian Front moved up to the Neisse River. Altogether, the three Soviet army groups had about 2.5 million men, 6,250 tanks, 7,500 aircraft, 41,600 artillery pieces and mortars, 3,255 truck-mounted Katyusha rocket launchers, and 95,383 motor vehicles.

The main Soviet objective would be the Seelöwe Heights, Germany's last major defensive line outside Berlin. Despite their overwhelming strength, it took nearly a million Soviet troops from 16 until 19 April to break through German defence lines held by about 100,000, with perhaps 10 per cent their number of tanks and artillery pieces. The German Eastern Front had now effectively ceased to exist, and the road to Berlin lay open for the vengeful Red Army.

THE FINAL CITADEL

In Berlin, SS Major Otto Günsche was appointed commander of the Government District, personally answerable to Hitler. His responsibility comprised Wilhelmstraße, Unter den Linden, Behrenstraße, Mauerstraße, Wilhelmplatz, Voss-Straße, and the Hermann-Göring-Straße as far as the Brandenburg Gate, as well as the Reichs Chancellery itself. To defend the Chancellery, Günsche had at his disposal the soldiers of the Guard Battalion of the Leibstandarte-SS, the Guard Regiment 'Grossdeutschland' and some elements of the SA 'Feldherrnhalle' Regiment, as well as the Führer Escort Battalion (now actually housed inside the Chancellery). There were also Security Police and SD elements, and Günsche could call upon several companies of the Berlin Volkssturm (home guard).

On Günsche's orders, a defensive ring was thrown around the Government District anchored on strongly fortified gun positions. The arches through the Brandenburg Gate were closed off, and machine guns were set up under the Quadriga on top of the gate. Goebbels' villa in the Hermann-Göring-Straße was not spared; embrasures were knocked through the garden walls and machine-gun nests were installed. In Voss-Straße the ruins of the bombed-out former Wertheim department store opposite the New Chancellery were made impassable with barbed wire and mines. All streets leading into Wilhelmstraße were defended with machine-gun nests and tank-traps, to prevent access to the Wilhelmplatz when necessary. There were fortified firing positions in the ruins of houses on the corners of Behrenstraße and Mauerstraße, and the Unter den Linden and Wilhelmstraße. Machine guns were installed on the roofs of the numerous ministries, and the Chancellery was fortified with particular care.

The balcony overlooking the Wilhelmplatz and up Wilhelmstraße now served as a machine-gun position, protected by its integral 8mm armour and covered with solid wooden railway-sleepers. Sandbags and obstacles were laid out ready in front of both the main entrances to the New Chancellery on Voss-Straße; the windows of the building were already barricaded and bristled with machine guns, and there were mortars and stocks of ammunition in the Chancellery garden. The number of sentry posts in the Chancellery was tripled, and more men were stationed at every entrance and exit.

While the capital was being prepared for defence by all means possible, the Nazi Party leaders were getting ready to flee. The signal to evacuate the highest state and Party administrators came from Martin Bormann; a long column of black limousines took them to safe hideaways in the area of Salzburg, Berchtesgaden and Bad Reichenhall in southern Germany. They had each received instructions to leave behind a skeleton staff of 10 to 15 experienced civil servants who could be evacuated later at short notice.

While the state administration was being moved to Bavaria, Hitler directed his butler Kannenberg to remove all remaining valuables and all his personal possessions from the Chancellery and to carry them to safety. Precious furniture, tapestries, carpets and paintings were taken to Schloss Moritzburg, which stood in a range of hills 15km (9m) from Dresden. Walter Erhardt, an SS lieutenant-colonel in Hitler's bodyguard, was ordered to take carvings and statues that had been acquired in Italy to the Stuttgart area. Hitler had his valet Linge and Adolf Dirr transport his own library by train to Bad Aussee near Salzburg, where it was housed in secure bunkers; it was there that Bormann also lodged the archives of the Munich branch of the Party Chancellery, which had been kept in the Brown House. Kannenberg personally transported to Bayreuth the state porcelain collection, used for official receptions and worth several million marks. The butler had said that he would soon be back, but he failed to return.

Friday 20 April 1945: the Soviet artillery of 1st Belarussian Front congratulated Hitler on his 56th birthday by shelling the centre of Berlin.

20 April 1945: One of the last images of Hitler, taken on his 56th birthday. Artur Axmann (right), head of the Hitlerjugend, presents Hitler Youth boys who had distinguished themselves in the defence of Berlin. The scene was filmed by the newsreel cameraman Walter Frentz in the Chancellery garden, in front of the terrace outside Hitler's study windows. (© Bildarchiv Preussischer Kulturbesitz)

During the day Hitler received birthday wishes by cable or in person from those who still were in Berlin. In the Chancellery garden, in front the terrace, Reichsführer-HJ Axmann gathered 20 boys that he was going to present to the Führer as 'warriors' – a sad contrast to the days when it was men like Günther Prien who stood proudly before their Führer. When Hitler came out of the bunker Axmann announced sharply, 'My Führer, your boys present arms'. Hitler took the salute, and said 'Heil, boys!', to which they replied, *'Heil, mein Führer!'*. Axmann had lined them up so that the youngest 'warrior' was standing on the left. Hitler gave each of them his hand and then delivered a short speech, in which he thanked them for their heroic deeds and claimed that the Reich would certainly win. With shaky hands he pinned the Iron Cross on each of their chests, pinching the cheeks of the youngest of them. After another exchange of salutes and *'Sieg Heils!'* Hitler went slowly back into his bunker, and Axmann packed his troop of teenagers off to front-line positions, to take their chances facing Soviet heavy tanks with shoulder-fired Panzerfaust rockets.

Heinz Linge arranged that all the Führer's personal belongings were packed, with the exception of the clothes he wore day in, day out. Some 40 to 50 chests were prepared for transport to the Obersalzberg, containing military documents that Hitler had received during the war from the OKW, OKH, Navy, Luftwaffe, and from Albert Speer. They had already been brought from the Wolfsschanze to the Chancellery when that headquarters was evacuated.

Bormann still hoped that Hitler would leave Berlin for the Obersalzberg, and on his orders Hitler's personal cook, Constanze Manziarly, packed the Führer's dietary provisions, leaving only a sufficient supply for a few days. Eva Braun's chambermaid Liesl continued to pester Linge as to whether she should pack or not. The whole day was filled with preparations to leave Berlin.

Saturday 21 April: The night of 20/21 April had been just like any other, loud with the work of RAF Bomber Command; but the Saturday morning was different. In pouring rain hundreds, perhaps thousands of cars, lorries and buses jammed the roads heading westwards out of the capital; Party leaders, ministers, civil servants, bankers, generals, indeed everyone who had the means and the connections was fleeing Berlin.

By now, Bogdanov's 2nd Guards Tank Army was about 50km (30 miles) north of Berlin and attacking the south-west of Werneuchen, and other Soviet units had reached the outer defence ring of the city. Hitler reacted by giving orders that showed that he had lost all grasp of military reality. In his mind the map-markings showing the last reported positions for armies, corps and divisions meant that they still had their established strengths in men and equipment; in reality they were simply battered remnants, scratched-together battle-groups lacking tanks, artillery, ammunition, transport air support. But still the Führer ordered that they should hold positions, and even mount counter-attacks.

As the Russians came closer and closer to Berlin, SS Major Günsche, until now nominal commander of the defence of the Government District, had a meeting with SS General Wilhelm Mohnke. Mohnke had commanded 1st SS Panzer Division 'Leibstandarte-SS Adolf Hitler' from August 1944 to the beginning of March 1945, and was presently on leave in Berlin after having been wounded. He offered to assemble and lead a battle-group of Waffen-SS men who were then in Berlin, including the Guard Battalion and odds and ends such as a training battalion and a convalescent company.[77] Günsche relayed the plan to Hitler, who agreed, whereupon Günsche ordered a massive stockpiling of weapons and ammunition in the Chancellery. In the shelters under the New Chancellery a huge depot of provisions was completed, and a field hospital was set up under the direction of the Chief Physician of the Berlin University Clinic, SS-Obersturmbannführer Professor Werner Haase.

The Joint Services HQ staff (OKW) at Zossen, known by the codename 'Maybach', left for Krampnitz at the start of a confused journey during which they were mistakenly shot up by

1945: Looking westwards down Voss-Straße, with the heavily damaged West wing of the Chancellery on the right and the Air Ministry on the left. (© Bildarchiv Preussischer Kulturbesitz)

Luftwaffe fighters. On 24 April they would leave Krampnitz for Neu-Ruppen; on the 28th they would be at Waren-Dobbin, on 1 May at Wismar, and from there, finally, they drove to Flensburg-Mürwik near the Danish border, where the government under Admiral Karl Dönitz was situated. The headquarters of the Kriegsmarine, 'Koralle', was also on the move; on 21 April they left Bernau north of Berlin, for Plön and eventually Flensburg.

Later that day Hitler decided that all dispensable staff should be taken to the Obersalzberg, as well as his personal effects and the military archive; only his immediate personal staff were to remain with him. His adjutants SS General Schaub and Luftwaffe Colonel von Below, and his personal pilot SS General Hans Baur, compiled lists of people to be flown to the Obersalzberg in aircraft of Baur's flight at Gatow – everyone was eager for a place on one of the Kondors or 'Aunt Judies'. When night fell on 21 April a long convoy of cars and lorries drove through the back gate of

the Chancellery into Hermann-Göring-Straße and headed for the airfield. Between 80 and 100 people flew to the Obersalzberg, including Hitler's personal adjutant Albert Bormann, his naval adjutant Admiral von Puttkamer, his dentist Hugo Blaschke, the secretaries Frau Wolf and Frau Schroeder, and some of the stenographers. The drivers who brought the cars back from Gatow that night reported that there were actual fist-fights over seats in the aircraft. From that moment, anyone who could leave Berlin did so, if necessary with falsified papers – even junior Chancellery staff destroyed their Party books and fled.

Linge despatched two other aircraft to the Obersalzberg; one carried 30–40 cases of Hitler's personal effects and dietary requirements, accompanied by the valet SS Captain Wilhelm Arndt and two servants. The second plane transported the 40–50 cases of documents which had been brought from the Wolfsschanze, escorted by SD agents. During the night a report came in from the

Obersalzberg that all the aircraft had landed safely except the one bearing Hitler's personal effects; Baur reported that it had been caught by American fighters, and forced to land near Cologne (it would be shot down in Saxony on the night of the 22nd/23rd).

As the capital was now under direct bombardment by Soviet artillery, Günsche arranged that the following should move out of the Old and New Chancelleries and take refuge in the New Chancellery shelters: Bormann, Burgdorf, Fegelein, Voss, Hewel, Lorenz, Zander, the adjutants Schaub, Albrecht, Below and Johannmeyer, the pilots Baur and Beetz, Rattenhuber, Högl and Schädle, and Dr Stumpfegger. General Krebs, Chief of the Army General Staff (OKH), was asked to stay near the Führer and was given a room in the New Chancellery bunker.

During the night of 21/22 April, Russian bombers attacked military targets in Berlin, and bombs also fell in the vicinity of the Chancellery.

Sunday 22 April: SS-Brigadeführer Mohnke appeared in the Chancellery to report his raising of the battle-group. Hitler ordered him to take over the defence of the whole Chancellery complex; Mohnke felt flattered, and remarked to Günsche that after the defeat at Lake Balaton 'the Führer didn't want to know about his Leibstandarte – now we'll show him he still has a Leibstandarte!'[78]

After living for weeks in the underground bunker Hitler was growing increasingly detached from reality. Sometimes at the situation conferences he fell into a rage when he realized that his orders to hold the lines and counter-attack had not brought the successes he had hoped for, and declared that the war was lost. On more than one occasion he burst into violent temper-tantrums when he was informed of the real situation in Berlin and the condition of the remaining German forces. During one such rage at a meeting with his military commanders he blamed the generals, and announced that he would stay in Berlin until the end. The stenographer Gerhard Herrgesell, captured by the Americans at the Obersalzberg, told *Time Magazine* correspondent Knauth what he had witnessed during the last recorded situation briefing held in the Führerbunker:

The decisive briefing which determined the fate of all of us began at 3 o'clock on the afternoon of 22 April and lasted until nearly 8 o'clock that evening. At this briefing Adolf Hitler declared that he wanted to die in Berlin. He repeated this ten or 20 times in various phrases. He would say: 'I will fall here', or 'I will fall before the Chancellery', or 'I must die here in Berlin.' He reasoned that the cause was irretrievably lost – in complete contrast to his previous attitude, which had always been: 'We will fight to the last tip of the German Reich.'

What reasons motivated his change of heart no one knows. . . . He had lost confidence in the Wehrmacht quite a while ago, saying that he had not gotten true reports, that bad news had been withheld from him. That afternoon he said that he was losing confidence in the Waffen-SS, for the first time. He had always counted on the Waffen-SS as elite troops which would never fail him. Now he pointed out a series of reports which he declared were false.

[The failure of some SS units to hold the Russians north of Berlin had apparently convinced Hitler that his crack troops had lost heart.] The Führer always maintained that no force, however well trained and equipped, could fight if it lost heart, and now he felt his last reserve was gone. During all this time participants in this conference were changing constantly. Hitler himself was generally composed. Every time he really began to get angry or excited, he would quickly get himself under control again. His face was flushed and red, however, and he paced the floor almost constantly, walking back and forth, sometimes smacking his fist into his hand. But of all the participants at all the conferences, the Führer was generally the one who kept his nerves best under control.

The really decisive conference took place in late afternoon. It lasted only about 15 minutes. Present were Hitler, Martin Bormann . . ., Field Marshal Wilhelm Keitel and Colonel-General Alfred Jodl. All others were sent away except the two stenographers.

Hitler again expressed his determination to stay in Berlin, and said he wanted to die there. He thought it would be the greatest service he could render to the honour of the German nation. In this conference his desire to stay in the Chancellery was violently opposed. Keitel spoke to him in really sharp terms, reminding him that his new attitude was contradictory to his former plans. Bormann supported Keitel no less strongly.

Jodl was a quiet man who spoke little, but when he spoke it was always clearly, frankly and to the point. Now he also came out strongly against Hitler. He declared very firmly that he, personally, would not stay in Berlin; he thought it was a mousetrap, and his job was to lead the troops, not stand with a flintlock in his hand defending the city and in the end dying in the rubble of its ruins.

When Keitel and Bormann saw that they could not move Hitler to change his mind, they said that in spite of his orders they would also stay. Hitler again ordered them to leave; in ten minutes, he said, the Russians might be before the Chancellery. Keitel and Bormann repeated that they would stay. Keitel added, 'We would never be able to face our wives and children if we left.'

Hitler then said that in two or three days, in a week at the very most, Berlin would be finished and the Chancellery taken. He said that he had considered what would happen after his own death. He gave an order to the other three men — it was not clear to whom he gave it, or whether he actually meant it as an order to one of them specifically. He said: 'You must go to southern Germany, form a government, and Göring will be my successor. Göring will negotiate.' Whether this last statement was an order or a prophecy, who can say. . . . The Führer was by now rather vague and uncertain, giving no direct orders, apparently preoccupied with the prospect of his own imminent death.

Jodl interjected that Germany still had some armies capable of action. He mentioned the Central Army Group under Field Marshal Schörner, which was disposed south of Berlin in the direction of Dresden, and the 12th Army of General Wenck, a newly formed army which was to stand against the Americans on the Elbe. Perhaps, said Jodl, these armies could change the course of events around Berlin. Hitler evinced little interest; he gave no orders, shrugged his shoulders and said: 'You do whatever you want' . . .

During all this time, artillery fire on the Chancellery was increasing and even deep down in the cellar we could feel concussions shaking the building.

General Jodl did send orders that evening to General Walther Wenck's 12th Army to move towards Berlin and try to link up with the forces under General Heinrici. In some people's minds Wenck became the saviour who would retrieve the situation even now.

Even as the Thousand-Year Reich was collapsing around them, arch-conspirators such as General Burgdorf, Martin Bormann and Joseph Goebbels were still manipulating their colleagues, and even Hitler himself. General Reymann, the commander of the Berlin Defence Area, was their new victim. By 21 April Goebbels, as Reich Commissioner for Berlin, had ordered that no man capable of bearing arms could leave the city; the only person who could issue an exemption was Reymann. With the Soviet encirclement of Berlin nearing completion, remaining senior Party officials – who in the past had bitterly attacked the Army for retreating – now rushed to Reymann's headquarters in search of the necessary passes to leave. This infuriated Goebbels, while Reymann was quite happy to see the back of some 2,000 useless 'armchair warriors'.

Goebbels, supported by Burgdorf, then convinced Hitler that the general had not been a good choice; Reymann was accused of defeatism and relieved of command, to be replaced by the newly promoted General Ernst Kaether – who was himself replaced before he could even take up his post. By the end of that day, when the first Soviet units were entering the suburbs of Berlin, Hitler declared he would personally take command of the city's defences.

Monday 23 April: At the front, the 1st Belarussian and 1st Ukrainian army groups were threatening to encircle the capital; elements of the latter were also moving westwards and starting to engage Wenck's 12th Army as it moved north-east towards Berlin. Russian artillery began shelling the Government District. A number of shells hit armoured vehicles that Mohnke's men had parked in the Ehrenhof of the Chancellery, as well as barrels of fuel; several soldiers were killed or badly wounded.

General Keitel received permission to visit Wenck's 12th Army, with the excuse of strengthening the morale of the troops, and left the bunker. He never returned, despite the fact that he had just solemnly sworn never to leave the Führer. At the same time Major Lohse, commanding the Führer Signal Battalion, disappeared from the Chancellery without leave.[79]

A strip of territory about 15–20km (9–12 miles) wide was now the only link between Berlin and the rest of the Reich, and it might be cut at any moment. Bormann ordered his assistant Zander to use this route to send all the workers in the Party Chancellery, including his assistant Müller and his six secretaries, out by bus and general-purpose vehicles to seek refuge in the Obersalzberg. Only Zander and the 30-year-old secretary Else Krüger were to stay in Berlin (Krüger was a friend of Eva Braun). After Hitler's doctor, Morell, left by plane Goebbels moved into his room in the bunker, just opposite Hitler's.

Hitler, changing his mind over his decision to take personal command, appointed General Helmuth Weidling as commander of the Berlin Defence Area.

Göring, who had left Berlin for the Obersalzberg with trainloads of stolen art, was without any news from Hitler, and sent a telegram suggesting that the Führer's testament should now come into force; if Göring had not received a sign of life by 10pm, he would assume leadership of Germany. The Reichsmarschall would get his reply; Hitler considered Göring's behaviour as an attempted coup d'état, and sent a message by plane ordering his immediate arrest by the SS. (On 26 April, Göring was dismissed as commander-in-chief of the Luftwaffe, and stripped of his Party and all other official functions.) Another Party veteran who went his own way was Reichsführer-SS Himmler. Then in northern Germany, 'Loyal Heinrich' started communicating with the Western Allies through neutral intermediaries about peace negotiations. Informed of Himmler's treachery, Hitler ordered his arrest and execution. (Neither Göring nor Himmler would in fact be arrested.)

That evening Hitler summoned Otto Günsche into the conference room, where Goebbels and Bormann were already present. All three were leaning over a map of Berlin that was lying on the table; staring at it, Hitler informed Günsche that he had just been told that people in the northern districts of Berlin and in the working-class area of Weissensee had hung red or white flags out of their windows. German soldiers in certain places had started retreating without a fight, and many had already deserted. Hitler ordered Günsche to send in an SS detachment at once, and to shoot or hang any fleeing soldiers on the spot.

Günsche promptly put together two mobile squads made up of SS men from Hitler's personal bodyguard and Chancellery drivers. He ordered them to proceed to northern Berlin and drive fleeing officers and men back to the trenches; anyone who resisted was to be brought to the Chancellery. After a while both squads returned with a group of officers and men, who were hanged on Friedrichstraße station; placards on their chests read: 'I hang here because I did not carry out the Führer's orders!'.

Tuesday 24 April: Units of 1st Belarussian and 1st Ukrainian Fronts completed the encirclement of the city. Foreign Minister von Ribbentrop flew out of Berlin for Hamburg. Another passenger was Walter Frentz, the former cameraman for Leni Riefensthal and *Die Wöchenschau*; on 20 April, he had taken the last footage of Hitler when he went into the garden of the Chancellery to decorate Axmann's Hitler Youth boys.[80]

Hitler told Heinz Linge and Julius Schaub that all remaining documents in the Chancellery were to be burned. Linge brought suitcases while Hitler began to pull documents out of the safe in the bunker: papers that he had received from Keitel, Jodl and Dönitz or from OKH since he had moved his headquarters to Berlin, his personal correspondence, and also several bundles of 50RM and 100RM banknotes. Linge packed them all into four suitcases, and with the assistance of servants dragged these out into the Chancellery garden. There the contents were tipped out and sorted into several heaps outside the emergency exit, before being drenched in petrol and set on fire. The last to be added were military situation reports, and a part of the military archive that had been brought from the Wolfsschanze. Linge waited until he was certain that every scrap had been burned.

In the meantime Schaub emptied the five safes in Hitler's private apartment in the Old Chancellery: political and military papers since before the war, and personal correspondence – drafts personally corrected by Hitler before being sent to Mussolini, Antonescu, Pétain and others, and their replies. With the help of a soldier-servant, Corporal Mandtal, Schaub packed one large suitcase and had the papers carried out into the garden by SS men to be consigned to the flames. Hitler himself pulled out the last documents relating to his time in office to be fed into the fire.

When all the documents found in the Chancellery had been burned, Schaub reported to Hitler in Linge's presence. Hitler instructed Schaub to fly without delay to the Obersalzberg, where he was to burn all the documents he could find in three large armour-plated cupboards in the Berghof. He handed Schaub the keys to the safes at the Berghof, which he always carried with him. That night Schaub came to bid goodbye before leaving the bunker together with Corporal Mandtal, who was to accompany him. He told those who were staying behind, 'In a few days I shall be back'; no one believed him Schaub flew from Gatow airfield, which was already being shelled by the Russians, and which would fall to them the next day. He never returned to Berlin. The two remaining stenographers, Gerhard Herrgesell and Kurt Haagen, who had taken the minutes during the last briefings, left the capital with him; there was no need for them any more.[81]

Wednesday 25 April: Soviet units penetrated the S-Bahn defensive ring.[82]

In the evening, Lieutenant Kuhlmann reported to Admiral Voss in the Chancellery; he had been flown in from Flensburg with several Ju 52s filled with Navy volunteers. Landing on the East-West axis, several aircraft had crashed due to running into shell-craters, killing and wounding many of the sailors.[83] This so-called Naval Rifle Battalion was placed under Mohnke's command. Some other units had also arrived in the capital; from the Tempelhof area came Scandinavian veterans and raw replacements of the 11th SS Volunteer Armoured Infantry Division 'Nordland', commanded from that day by SS-Brigadeführer Krukenberg, bringing with him about 300 Frenchmen from the former SS Assault Brigade 'Charlemagne'.

General Weidling's forces to defend the capital included the remnants of several Army and Waffen-SS divisions, in all about 45,000 men.[84] These formations were severely depleted in manpower and equipment, and replacements recently scraped-up to fill out their ranks were unemployed Luftwaffe and Kriegsmarine personnel, who had been turned into infantrymen on paper but not by training. These troops were supplemented by Police, Hitler Youth teenagers, and Volkssturm units of middle-aged or elderly 'home guard' conscripts; the quality and quantity of their personnel, weapons and training varied enormously. Weidling organized the defences into eight sectors designated A to H, each one commanded by a general or a colonel, few of whom had any combat experience. SS General Gustav Krukenberg was appointed commander of Defence Sector C, the sector under the most pressure from the Soviet assault.

During the night of 25/26 April the Russians cut the last telephone cables linking Berlin with the outside. The only means of communication were now two not very reliable 100-watt radio sets, of which the antennae were repeatedly damaged by artillery fire.

Thursday 26 April: On this day the Red Army and the Western Allies shook hands at Torgau on the River Elbe, far to the west of Berlin.

At 7am, Soviet artillery launched a heavy bombardment of the Government District; the Chancellery, and even parts of the underground levels, were struck by a storm of heavy shells. The roof of the 'Kannenberggang' passageway from the New Chancellery to the Führerbunker was smashed in several places, and large puddles formed on the floor; these had to be crossed, with difficulty, on planks. Through the holes in the roof of this now-sinister tunnel dark clouds of smoke and the burning roof of the Chancellery could be seen.

The fighting continued all round Berlin. The 8th Guards Army – commanded by General Chuikov, the hero of Stalingrad – and the 1st Guards Tank Army fought their way through the southern suburbs and attacked Tempelhof airport, just inside the S-Bahn defensive ring.

Friday 27 April: The two remnant SS divisions defending the south-east, facing five Soviet armies, were forced to pull back towards the centre and take up new defensive positions around Hermannplatz. SS General Krukenberg informed General Krebs that within 24 hours his 'Nordland' Division would have to fall back to Sector Z – for *Zentrum*, the centre.

A strange noise joined the more usual monotone humming of the ventilators of the Führerbunker. Mechanic Hans Hentschel told Linge that it was caused by the heavy fires in the garden sucking in oxygen and causing a wind to blow up – a miniature firestorm. The wooden barracks, to which drivers and servants had been moved when Hitler's headquarters took over the Chancellery, were also burning.

The Soviet advance on the city centre was from the following main directions:

From the south-east, along the Frankfurter-Allee, but currently halted at the Alexanderplatz.

From the south, along Sonnen-Allee, but halted north of the Belle-Alliance-Platz, and also near the Potsdamer Platz.

From the north, Soviet units had arrived outside the Reichstag building.

The fighting was heaviest at the Reichstag, the Moltke Bridge, the Alexanderplatz, and the Havel bridges at Spandau, with house-to-house and hand-to-hand combat. As always in street-fighting, the attackers paid with heavy casualties for almost every yard they gained.

The protective ring around the Government District held by Mohnke's battle-group of perhaps 3,500 men had been attacked by Soviet tanks at several points.[85] These were exerting particularly heavy pressure on the Spree bridges, on the Tirpitzufer and Potsdamer-Straße, the Hallesche Tor and the Lustgarten. Hitler ordered Mohnke to blow up the bridges over the Spree.

That evening, two SS servants were married. The wedding was celebrated at 7pm in the common room of the old bunker where Hitler's bodyguard had their quarters. The couple were married by the State Secretary of the Propaganda Ministry, SS General Dr Werner Naumann; the witnesses were SS Majors Linge and Schädl; everyone wore steel helmets and had holstered pistols at their belts. The wedding guests were Hitler's adjutants, the officers of his bodyguard and the SD detail, as well as the other SS batmen. Naumann declared solemnly that the exchange of vows was taking place at a memorable time, under a hail of shells from the Russian artillery in a Berlin in the throes of battle; but the relief of the capital was nigh, and the young couple had many years of untroubled fortune ahead of them.

After the wedding Linge gave a meal for the newly-weds; champagne and cognac followed, the reception turned into a drinking-bout, and dancing and merriment continued until the next morning, despite the fact that during that night of 27/28 April the bombardments redoubled in intensity. The vibration of the uninterrupted pounding of the Chancellery above could be felt through the earth and inside the concrete block of the Führerbunker. The ceiling of the Vorbunker, less thick, was in danger of collapsing under the shelling. Water trickled into all parts of the already damaged Kannenberggang, through the gaps torn by rockets; dust and smoke filtered in through the ventilators throughout the complex. The emergency lighting, powered by generators, flickered on and off, sometimes throwing the bunker into darkness and disarray. Filth piled up everywhere; waste matter was no longer removed, and people tried to sleep on mattresses jumbled together in the corridors.

Saturday 28 April: At 9 am, Mohnke phoned Günsche; the Russians were attacking at the Hallesche Tor, fierce battles were raging on the Belle-Alliance-Platz and on the corner of Wilhelmstraße. Mohnke added that the telephone connections between his command post and his units had been broken; he was sending out runners, and hoped soon to have a clearer picture of the situation.

The Red Army were within 1,200 or 1,300 yards of the Chancellery; checked by fierce resistance, the leading troops now attacked Gleisdreieck and Anhalt station. The massively constructed public buildings provided Mohnke's troops with strong fortresses; infantry alone could not drive them out, and the rubble in the streets hampered the Soviet tanks and self-propelled guns.

Sunday 29 April: In the early hours of the morning, troops of the Soviet 3rd Shock Army crossed the Moltke Bridge and started to spread through the surrounding streets and buildings. At first the infantry lacked the supporting fire they needed for assaults on the defended buildings, including the Interior Ministry; the damaged bridges would have to be repaired before heavy weapons could cross them and come up in support.

In the Führerbunker, some people were no longer aware whether it was day or night. At 1am, Councillor Walter Wagner was brought to the Führerbunker, where he was told he was to marry Adolf Hitler to Eva Braun. Bormann and Goebbels were their witnesses; and 30 minutes later Bormann, Goebbels and his wife, the secretaries Christian and Junge, Generals Krebs and Burgdorf, Colonel von Below, Otto Günsche and Hitler's dietician Manzialy got together to celebrate the happy occasion. Hitler only stayed with them for half an hour, before withdrawing to his study accompanied by Traudl Junge to dictate his private and political wills.

On the first page of the former the underlined heading read '*Mein privates Testament*'; it was dated 29 April 1945, 4am. At the end were five signatures; the first was small and tightly wound, like a compressed thunderbolt: Adolf Hitler. The others were more expansive and boldly ambitious: the witnesses Martin Bormann, Joseph Goebbels and General Krebs.[86] Apart from Krebs' the same signatures witnessed the considerably longer '*Mein politsches Testament*', in which Hitler railed against his generals, and expelled Himmler and Göring from the Nazi Party. He appointed Grand Admiral Karl Dönitz as Reich President and Goebbels as Chancellor, but abolished the post of Führer (controlling to the last, he went on to name an entire 17-member cabinet).

In his will, Hitler explained that he preferred ending his own life to being paraded around like a zoo-exhibit. He wanted his paintings donated to a picture gallery in Linz, and distributed some personal mementos to his secretaries, particularly Frau Winter. 'As executor, I appoint my most faithful Party comrade, Martin Bormann. He is given full legal authority to hand over to my relatives . . . especially to my wife's mother . . . everything which is . . . necessary to maintain a petty-bourgeois standard of living.' His final written words commanded Germany's future leaders to 'mercilessly resist the universal poisoner of all nations, international Jewry.'

At dawn the Soviets pressed on with their assault in the south-east. After very heavy fighting they managed to capture the Gestapo headquarters on Prinz-Albrecht-Straße, but a Waffen-SS counter-attack later forced them to withdraw from the ruined building. To the south-west, they attacked and crossed the Landwehr canal.

At 8am, General Burgdorf ordered Major Willi Johannmeyer, Army adjutant to the Führer, to take Hitler's will to Field Marshal Ferdinand Schörner.[87] Bormann chose his aide, SS-Standartenführer Wilhelm Zander, to take a copy to Dönitz in Flensburg, while Goebbels sent Heinz Lorenz, Hitler's Chief Press Secretary, to the Brown House in Munich.[88] At noon on the 29th, Hitler's former orderly officer Freiherr Bernd Freytag von Loringhoven, his former ADC Captain Gerhard Boldt and General Burgdorf's

Looking north-west from the roof of the West wing of the Chancellery, towards the domed
Reichstag *building in the distance. On the left are the destroyed barrack blocks along*
Hermann-Göring-Straße. In the garden behind them large holes can be seen, blown in the roofs of
the underground garages and workshops. In centre foreground, note that the wall dividing the
barrack gardens from those of the Chancellery has been reinforced with loopholed pillboxes. To the
right of the wall is the line of pillars that once supported the roof of the pergola.

ADC Oberstleutnant Rudolf Weiss were sent to General Wenck of 12th Army in a last attempt to convince him to advance towards Berlin; each carried copies of both of Hitler's wills.

Communications had now become nearly impossible, and at 4.52pm Admiral Voss warned Flensburg by radio that all connections were broken. By nightfall troops of the Soviet 8th Guards Army had advanced from the Zoo into the Tiergarten, and their tanks had reached the Reichstag. In Prinz-Albrecht-Straße, between the Anhalt station and the Potsdamer-Platz, Red Army tanks were only 300–500 meters from the Chancellery. Battles were being fought in Friedrichstraße, Prinzenstraße and the Spittel-markt.

Monday 30 April: Soviet troops had repaired the urgently needed bridges; artillery was brought up

to support the infantry, and these launched the attack on the Reichstag at 6am.

At the Führerbunker, General Weidling arrived with no good news. Ammunition was running so low that they would barely be able to supply the troops during one more night. Hitler was already aware of the situation, since at around 6am Mohnke had asked for a private audience, at which he informed the Führer that the troops defending the Government District only had ammunition for another 24 hours at most.

Supported by 8.8cm guns mounted on top of the Zoo flak tower, Waffen-SS troops were still defending the Reichstag stubbornly against the Soviet 79th Rifles Corps. Inside, the gutted building still looked as it had done after the fire in 1934, providing the defenders with excellent concealed positions in the rubble. Fierce room-to-room fighting ensued; in the end, it would take the

Russians nearly 48 hours to capture the entire building.

Hitler gave General Weidling permission to attempt a breakout through the Soviet lines. Then, at some time after 2pm on 30 April, he and Eva Braun committed suicide in their sitting-room. Their bodies were cremated a few steps from the emergency exit into the Chancellery garden – which was as far into the open air as anyone dared to go.[89]

Tuesday 1 May: With Soviet troops closing in, the surviving defenders were forced back into a shrinking perimeter in the Government District. At about 4am General Krebs – a former military attaché in Moscow, who spoke fluent Russian – went to meet General Chuikov of the Soviet 8th Guards Army. When Krebs informed the defender of Stalingrad of Hitler's death, Chuikov left him practically speechless by replying that he already knew of it. Krebs tried to negotiate a surrender in Berlin alone, but the Russians insisted on unconditional surrender.

Without the authorization to agree, Krebs returned to the bunker. Goebbels committed suicide with his wife after having murdered their own six children. With the last major political obstacle removed, General Weidling accepted the terms of unconditional surrender of his garrison, though he still chose to delay it until early the next morning so as to allow time to plan breakouts.

At 8pm, Günsche, Linge, Schädl and Kempka went to Mohnke's command post. Exhausted soldiers of his battle-group lay everywhere in the corridors and rooms of the New Chancellery bunker. Axmann, Naumann, Albrecht, Rattenhuber and several officers from the battle-group had already found their way to the meeting. Mohnke read out the order to escape, and specified in what stages the Chancellery was to be evacuated.

The first group was to be led by Mohnke himself and would include Günsche, Hewel, Admiral Voss, Frau Christian, Frau Junge, Fräulein Krüger and Fräulein Manziarly, as well as Hitler's Escort Company under the command of SS-Obersturmführer Doose. The second group, led by Naumann, would be composed of Bormann, Schacht, the remaining officials of the

Berlin Nazi Party, and a Volkssturm battalion from the Propaganda Ministry.

The third group, headed by Kempka, was to include Linge, the soldier-servants, Hitler's personal SD bodyguard and the Chancellery drivers. A fourth group would be commanded by Hitler's personal adjutant, SS-Brigadeführer Albrecht, and would consist of the other adjutants. The fifth group, commanded by Rattenhuber, would comprise Baur, Beetz, Högl and members of the SD.

The sixth and last group would be led by Axmann, and was to be composed of 200 Berlin HJ-boys whom he had brought into the bunker a few days before to get Hitler out of Berlin. When Hitler had refused their services, Axmann kept them for his own use.

Some other soldiers and civil servants joined these groups; needless to say, their organization quickly dissolved in practice. In all, up to 2,000 people, most of them armed, fled from the Chancellery complex. Others, such as Generals Krebs and Burgdorf, chose to stay behind.

Wednesday 2 May 1945: General Helmuth Weidling unconditionally surrendered Berlin to General Vasily Chuikov. Troops of the Soviet 248th and 301st Rifles Divisions entered the Chancellery, where they were met by resistance from some remaining SS guards who clearly felt they had nothing to loose.

One of the last people to have stayed in the Chancellery and the bunker was Erna Flegel, a German Red Cross nurse who had been with Hitler during the final weeks of the war. A former nurse on the Eastern Front, she was asked whether she would be interested in a position in the Reichs Chancellery; used to carrying out orders, she agreed. On arriving at the Chancellery she was still impressed by its size and opulence.

After the attempted breakout Sister Flegel stayed at her post; she would recall:

We knew the Russians were approaching. As we were in the bunker another nurse phoned me up and [warned me]. Then they turned up in the Reichs Chancellery. It was a huge building complex. The Germans were transported away

6 May 1945: General Weidling is forced to play-act, for the Soviet cameramen, his emergence from the Chancellery air raid shelters to surrender. This shows clearly one of the hydraulic doors in the pavement of Voss-Straße in front of the Mittelbau – *see also page 45. (© Bildarchiv Preussischer Kulturbesitz)*

and we were left. The Russians treated us very humanely. They came to the entrance and we negotiated with them. First of all they sent someone to talk to us and to have a look round. By this stage there were only six or seven of us left, no more. They looked here and there. They were selected personnel and they behaved quite decently. They found everything stored downstairs. Anyone who needed anything went downstairs. The Russians respected this. The Germans were no longer responsible for anything. It worked. I stayed in the bunker for another six to ten days.

You could feel that the Third Reich was coming to an end. The radios stopped working and it was impossible to get information.

Erna Flegel and the senior electrical mechanic Johannes Hentschel were among the last people to leave the bunker.

The nominal Dönitz government, established near the Danish border, unsuccessfully sought a separate peace with the Western Allies. Between 4 and 8 May 1945, the remaining German armed forces throughout Europe surrendered unconditionally.

Epilogue

Berlin's end came two years and three months after the final destruction of the 6th Army at Stalingrad; 16 days after the Soviet armies lunged across the Oder for Hitler's capital, and 12 days after they reached its streets.

Berlin, once so elegant and proud, was a pounded corpse of a city. All that was left were ruins, craters, burned-out tanks, smashed guns, tramcars riddled with holes, half-demolished trenches, litters of spent shells, fresh graves, corpses still awaiting burial, masses of white flags, and crowds of glum and hungry inhabitants. About 90 per cent of the city centre was destroyed. The Friedrichstraße was impossible to pass on foot as the pavement had sunk into the ground; the ceiling of the underground railway tunnel, which ran just below the street, had caved in.

Summer 1945: American WACs walk down Wilhelmstraße past the Führerbalkon. *The 8mm armour plate incorporated in its construction made it a useful defensive position for the Chancellery during the last days' fighting; with wooden railway sleepers added for overhead protection, three of Mohnke's machine-gun crews could cover the length of Wilhelmstraße and the whole Wilhelmplatz. (© Ullstein: 00074831)*

Impact of a Soviet shell on the stonework of one of the portals on Voss-Straße. Above, note the gaps in the ceiling where mosaic decorative panels were originally installed. (© Bildarchiv Preussischer Kulturbesitz)

May 1945: An armoured self-propelled assault gun abandoned in front of the Mittelbau, *with the damaged West wing beyond. (© Ullstein: 00268144)*

Summer 1945: Curious visitors gaze at the collapsed marble floor of the Runder Saal, *which received a direct hit during air raids on the Government District. (© Bildarchiv Preussischer Kulturbesitz)*

Summer 1945: The Wilhelmplatz seen from inside the first floor of the Siedler extension, with the Führer's balcony – now stripped of its timber armour – outside the window.

The Thousand-Year Reich is in ruins after just 12 years, and a German officer lies dead and stripped of his boots at the Presidential Chancellery portal in the East wing on Voss-Straße. The litter of small boxes on the steps around his corpse apparently held medals. (© Ullstein: 00080492)

LEFT: *A* Trümmerfrau *or 'rubble woman' – one of the scores of thousands of women right across the former Reich who cleared the debris of Germany's ruined cities with their bare hands, as a first step towards the rebuilding of their country. (© Bundesarchiv: 183-S94178)*

BELOW: *Two of the patient 'rubble-women' take a break for a precious cigarette beside the ornamental pool in the Chancellery garden. They are sitting at its south-west corner, and the viewpoint is to the north-east. Above their heads in the background can be seen the reception hall behind the Old Chancellery; immediately left of the single tree above the left-hand woman is the southern of the two turret-shaped ventilation-shaft heads for the Führerbunker. Hidden beyond it is the domed block housing the emergency exit, outside which Hitler and Eva Brauin were cremated. (© Bildarchiv Preussischer Kulturbesitz)*

1946: A view from roughly north-west to south-east, showing the west face of the new reception hall built behind the Old Chancellery, with the Vörbunker *beneath it. The* Haupt- *or* Führerbunker *proper lay below the open space to the right; in the foreground is the northern and much smaller of the two turret-shaped air-shaft heads. The domed emergency exit block – called the 'tower-house' in Kempka's testimony in Appendix 4 – lay behind and to the right of where the photographer stood to take this view. (© Bildarchiv Preussischer Kulturbesitz)*

Soviet officers show Prime Minister Winston Churchill and Foreign Minister Anthony Eden the Great Reception Hall of the Chancellery, its walls now covered with Russian graffiti. It is hardly surprising that after fighting all the way from the Caucasus and the Volga at such catastrophic cost, every Red Army frontovik *who got the chance wanted to leave his mark on the beast's lair. (© Bildarchiv Preussischer Kulturbesitz)*

The Marmorgalerie *in the post-war years, stripped bare of everything including the marble facings from the walls.*

1947: The Mosaikssaal, *looking westwards towards the* Runder Saal. *(© Ullstein: 00107401)*

1950: Narrow-gauge tracks were laid all over Berlin, allowing trains of mine-trucks to collect and carry away the debris gathered by the 'rubble-women'. This one runs through the Chancellery gardens; the viewpoint is perhaps towards the south-west. (© Bundesarchiv: 183-0806-0003)

The end of Hitler's sick world: These two children playing in the overgrown Chancellery garden are sitting on the remains of the globes that used to stand in his office and the State Cabinet Room. (© Bundesarchiv: 183-M1204-316)

The Tiergarten was burning, its trees crackling and writhing in the flames. The Reichstag was smoking, and the Chancellery was still burning. The windows were blocked with heaps of books, with the barrels of abandoned machine guns sticking out between them. Inside, the fire was spreading, floors were glowing with heat and about to collapse. Across the street flames also rose from Göring's Air Ministry; it was impossible to go inside its thick stone walls, but beneath it the gigantic air raid shelter was untouched.

Through this smouldering shambles, columns of German soldiers – mostly very young or elderly – shuffled forward to throw down their arms at collection points. Men with grey, stubbly beards crept out of cellars, subways and dugouts carrying white flags; they were gathered up like sheep, and trudged silently out of the city under the submachine guns of Soviet guards.

But spring was in the air, the shelling had stopped, and despite everything some people had the feeling of waking from a nightmare. Here, as in every other city in the Reich, the *Trümmerfrauen* – 'rubble women' – patiently began the immense task of clearing up the debris. Before the week was out, Radio Berlin was back on the air. The Chancellery was not emptied only by souvenir hunters, but also by Berliners who used its materials to restore their ruined homes. The plundering reached such proportions that the Allies had to put up warning signs forbidding it.

Allied politicians, senior generals, officers and privates – and even German citizens – came to Berlin to gaze at what was left of Hitler's New Reichs Chancellery. In July 1945, Winston Churchill and Anthony Eden came to pay a visit; looking over the ruins of the Old Chancellery, Eden waved toward one bomb-blasted room and recalled, 'I had dinner with Hitler just over there in 1935'. At this, Churchill growled 'You certainly paid for that dinner, Anthony'.

Little by little, the Russians and the new Berlin city council stripped the marble and granite from the Chancellery to build three monuments: a war memorial in the Tiergarten (1945/46), a Russian commemorative memorial for the military cemetery at Treptow Park (1946/49), and a monument in the Schönholzer Heide (1947/49). In 1950, the underground station at the Thalmannplatz, now Mohrenstraße, was restored with the last marble slabs from the Chancellery. The Breker statues from the Ehrenhof were melted down and the bronze reused to cast the figures of Russian soldiers that stand at the Tiergarten monument.

In his memoirs, Albert Speer wrote that Hitler liked to say that the purpose of Speer's buildings was to transmit his time and its spirit to posterity. His architecture had to speak to the conscience of future generations of Germans, so Speer's theory of 'ruin value' pleased Hitler. Monumental Party buildings would be constructed with natural materials such as granite and marble, so that they would decline gently over centuries into ruins like their Roman and Greek models.

Hitler's *Neue Reichkanzlei*, the first official construction of his new 'Germania', would last just over six years. It did not decay in beauty into an ivy-covered ruin, but was blasted by British bombs and Soviet artillery. After the war, first the Russians and then the German Democratic Republic demolished Albert Speer's New Chancellery stone by stone, and its very last remains were erased in 1950.

Appendix 1
Guarding the Führer

From the start of Adolf Hitler's political career he was always guarded by groups raised especially for that purpose. At first these were just a handful of men, but they later grew into whole units (indeed, by extension, into an entire armoured corps that claimed this lineage).

One of the units raised to protect the Führer on his travels was the *SS-Begleitkommando des Führers* (the Führer's Escort Command); this was the team immediately responsible for his life, while other units provided outer rings of protec-tion. It was composed of carefully selected SS men, each of them personally approved by Hitler himself. Formed on 29 February 1932, the original unit comprised eight men: Franz Schädle, Bruno Gesche, Erich Kempka, August Körber, Adolf Dirr, Kurt Gildisch, Willy Herzberger and Bodo Gelzenleuchter.

In 1937 they numbered 17 men; by 1941 they had 35, and by 15 January 1943 they numbered 31 SS officers with 112 men. Thirty-three of them acted as personal escorts to the Führer, rotating in

Lieutenant-Colonel Gerhard Engel, left, Hitler's Army adjutant from March 1938 to October 1943, photographed with SS Colonel Johann Rattenhuber of the SD, who commanded the Chancellery security detail throughout Hitler's years in power. (© Ullstein: 00458699)

shifts of 11 men; the rest served as his valets, drivers and orderlies. The unit was commanded successively by:

Bodo Gelzenleuchter (29 February 1932– ?)

SS-Hauptsturmführer Willy Herzberger (? –11 April 1933)

SS-Obersturmführer Kurt Gildisch (11 April 1933–15 June 1934)

SS-Obersturmführer Bruno Gesche (15 June 1934–January 1945)

SS-Untersturmführer Franz Schädle (January 1945–8 May 1945)

From 15 March 1933, this team was supported when he was in Bavaria by the *Führerschutzkommando*. Made up mainly of Bavarian former Criminal Police officers, this could serve within the borders of Bavaria only.

On 1 August 1935 the Führerschutzkommando was absorbed into the *Reichssicherheitsdienst* or SD. This, the intelligence service of the SS, had its beginnings in 1931 when the man who would be its chief, Reinhard Heydrich (a former naval intelligence officer) persuaded Himmler of its wide possibilities, and Himmler's first target for a take-over was the Bavarian political police. As the SD the service hugely expanded its size and areas of activity, from internal security in Germany to death-squads in the occupied Eastern territories; but it remained responsible for the Führer's protection, and later for that of the other leaders of the Third Reich, both at home and in some occupied territories.

According to Himmler, the members of the protection department had to be 'tried and trusted National Socialists, and furthermore excellent criminal police officers of unconditional reliability, utmost conscientiousness in fulfilment of their duties, good manners and physical dexterity', while its tasks included personal security, investigation of assassination plans, surveillance of locations before the arrival of the protected person, and checking of buildings as well as personnel.

The protection department could request assistance from other organizations, and took command of all local police detailed for Hitler's protection during his visits to a city.

During the war the OKW gave them the status of secret military police, and the unit was referred to as the *Reichssicherheitsdienst Gruppe Geheime Feldpolizei*. They could now demand help from the regular Feldgendarmerie as well as any other troops, enter any military building, wear the uniform of any branch, and so forth. The officers were sworn in at the Feldherrnhalle in Munich by Himmler in the presence of Hitler, and they took the Wehrmacht oath until 1936. On 1 May 1937 all SD officers were made SS members; only those who were eligible for SS membership could join the SD, and all officers had to present proof that they were of 'unsullied' German blood.

The commander of the Führer's SD protection team – *Sicherheits-Kontrolldienst Reichskanzlei* – from 15 March 1933 until 8 May 1945 was SS-Standartenführer (later SS-Gruppenführer) Johann Rattenhuber. The team started with a strength of 45 men, and numbered 50 in 1940. At first they wore black SS uniforms, but on the outbreak of war the whole SD changed to field-grey. When serving in the Chancellery they carried 7.65mm Walther PPK automatic pistols and flashlights. Their responsibilities included patrolling the Reichs Chancellery, the Presidential Chancellery, the Führer's Chancellery and the SA leadership offices, and keeping under surveillance any construction and repair work in the building. They provided doormen and other surveillance personnel, supervising and checking all persons in the Chancellery area, including the other security services.

In 1944 SD protection teams were also responsible for the safety of Hermann Göring, Joachim von Ribbentrop, Heinrich Himmler, Josef Goebbels, Wilhelm Frick, Karl Dönitz, Ernst Kaltenbrunner, Robert Ley, Erich Koch, and also Hans Frank in Prague, Artur Seyss-Inquart in The Hague, Josef Terboven in Oslo and Werner Best in Copenhagen. Apart from the Reichs Chancellery they guarded the residences in Munich and Berchtesgaden (Obersalzberg).

Another unit that served close to Hitler was the *Führer Begleit Bataillon* (Führer Escort Batallion). This was a combination of Luftwaffe personnel detached from the Regiment General Göring and Army personnel from the Wachregiment Berlin (from April 1939 retitled Wachregiment 'Grossdeutschland'). While the SS and SD were responsible for escort services and protection inside Hitler's headquarters and residences, the Führer Begleit Bataillon defended the area in and around the grounds of headquarters. After the oubreak of war this unit grew steadily, eventually reaching (nominally) the strength of a full division which was deployed to the front.

Security at the Chancellery itself was thus provided by members of the SS and SD, but also by the Gestapo (plain clothes Secret State Police) and Security Police – all these being elements of Himmler's SS empire, and all except the Waffen-SS being controlled by Heydrich's (later Kaltenbrunner's) Reich Main Security Office or RSHA. There was also, though to a lesser and subordinate extent, an SA presence, due to the location of that organization's leadership in the former Borsig Palace at Voss-Straße No.2.

The entrances of Voss-Straße Nos.4 and 6 were always guarded by pairs of sentries from the Leibstandarte-SS or the Army's Berlin-based Wachregiment 'Grossdeutschland', while that at No.2 was guarded by men of the only SA unit permitted to bear arms, the 'Feldherrnhalle' Regiment. Around the building, on the pavement, Gestapo and Police agents would patrol day and night. From 21 September 1940 the pavements in front of the New Chancellery in the Voss- and Wilhelmstraße were closed to pedestrians.

Inside the building, more Waffen-SS sentries were on fixed guard while SD men patrolled the rooms, corridors and garden; to enter the underground garages one needed to show an SS sentry a special green pass signed by Erich Kempka, chief of the motor pool. The use of passes was so widespread – issued in several colours by each department in the Chancellery – that it had to be revised several times. Workmen inside the building had to be followed by SD or SS guards.

In the last months of the war the SD-Kontrolldienst and SS-Begleitkommando moved with Hitler into the bunker.

Appendix 2
Hitler's Personal Staff

Persönliche Adjutanten des Führers:

SA-Obergruppenführer Wilhelm Brückner (Chief Adjutant, 1934–40)

SS-Obergruppenführer Julius Schaub* (Adjutant, 1922–40; Chief Adjutant, 1940–45)

NSKK-Gruppenführer Albert Bormann (Chief of Hitler's Private Chancellery, 1931–45)

NSKK-Brigadeführer Fritz Wiedemann (Adjutant, 1935–39)

Chefadjutant der Wehrmacht beim Führer & Chef des Heeresperssonalamtes:

General der Infanterie Rudolf Schmundt (Chief Military Adjutant, 1938–44)

General der Infanterie Wilhelm Burgdorf* (Chief Military Adjutant, 1944–45)

France, summer 1940: Hitler poses with his immediate entourage and senior officers of Joint Services Supreme Command (OKW). (Left to right, front row) *Wilhelm Brückner, Otto Dietrich, General Keitel (Chief of OKW), Hitler, General Jodl (Chief of Operations, OKW), Martin Bormann, Colonel von Below, Heinrich Hoffmann.* (Middle row) *General Bodenschatz, General Schmundt, SS General Wolff, Dr Morel, SS Captain Hans Georg Schulze.*
(Back row) *Lieutenant-Colonel Engel, Dr Brandt, Admiral von Puttkamer, Walther Hewel, (unknown), SS General Julius Schaub, SS Lieutenant Wünsche. (Library of Congress)*

Adjutant der Wehrmacht (Heer) beim Führer:

Oberstleutnant Gerhard Engel (Adjutant, 03.1938-10.1943)

Oberstleutnant Heinrich Borgmann (Adjutant, 09.1943-03.1945)

Oberstleutnant Erik von Amsberg (Adjutant, 07.1944-10.1944)

Major Willi Johannmeyer* (Adjutant, 04.1945-05.1945)

Adjutant der Wehrmacht (Luftwaffe) beim Führer:

Oberst Nicolaus von Below* (Adjutant, 1937-04.1945)

Adjutant der Wehrmacht (Kriegsmarine) beim Führer:

Korvettenkapitän Karl-J. von Puttkamer (Adjutant, 1935–38)

Leutnant Alwin-Broder Albrecht (Adjutant, 1938–39)

Konteradmiral Karl-J. von Puttkamer* (Adjutant, 1939–45)

Vizeadmiral Hans-Erich Voss* (Adjutant, 1943–45)

Persönliche SS Adjutanten des Führers:

SS-Sturmbannführer Fritz Darges (Adjutant, 1943–44)

SS-Sturmbannführer Otto Günsche* (Adjutant, 1943–45)

SS-Obersturmführer Ludwig Bahls (Orderly Officer, 1937–38)

SS-Hauptsturmführer Hans Pfeiffer (Orderly Officer, 1939–42)

SS-Obersturmführer Max Wünsche (Orderly Officer, 1939–40)

SS-Hauptsturmführer Hans-Georg Schulze (Orderly Officer, 1940–41)

SS-Obersturmbannführer Richard Schulze (Orderly Officer, 1942–44)

SS-Gruppenführer Johann Rattenhuber* (Chief of SD security detail, 1933–45)

SS-Obersturmbannführer Bruno Gesche (Chief of Führerbegleitkommando, 1934–45)

(* = with Hitler in the Führerbunker)

Miscellaneous:

SS-Obersturmbannführer Karl W. Krause (Chief Valet, 1933–39)

SS-Obersturmbannführer Heinz Linge* (Valet, 1933–39; Chief Valet, 1939–45)

SS-Obersturmführer Hans Junge (Personal Valet, 1937–43)

SS-Brigadeführer Julius Schreck (Driver, 1925–36)

SS-Obersturmbannführer Erich Kempka* (Driver & Chief of Motor Pool, 1936–45)

SS-Gruppenführer Hans Baur* (Chief Pilot, 1920s-1945)

SS-Obersturmbannführer Karl Beetz* (Co-Pilot)

SS-Gruppenführer Karl Brandt (Hitler's personal doctor, 1933–45)

SS Commissioned Ranks

Throughout this text, covering the 12-year history of the Third Reich, various personalities are naturally mentioned in different ranks. Since those closest to Hitler were often given extraordinarily senior SS ranks for their apparent functions, the following approximate table of English equivalents and German abbreviations may be helpful to readers.

SS-Untersturmführer (SS-Ustuf) = Second lieutenant

SS-Obersturmführer (SS-Ostuf) = First lieutenant

SS-Hauptsturmführer (SS-Hstuf) = Captain

SS-Sturmbannführer (SS-Stubaf) = Major

SS-Obersturmbannführer (SS-Ostubaf) = Lieutenant colonel

SS-Standartenführer (SS-Staf) = Colonel

General ranks:

SS-Oberführer (SS-Oberf) = Brigadier

SS-Brigadeführer (SS-Brigaf) = Major general

SS-Gruppenführer (SS-Gruf) = Lieutenant general

SS-Obergruppenführer (SS-Ogruf) = General

SS-Oberstfruppenführer (SS-Obstgruf) = Colonel general

Appendix 3
Dramatis personae

Arndt, Wilhelm 'Willi' (1913–45) Studied at a hotel school; entered the Leibstandarte-SS, and became a personal servant to Hitler from 1943. Died in plane crash near Börnersdorf, Saxony, 22 April 1945.

Axmann, Artur (1913–96) Studied law; founded the first Hitler Youth group in Westphalia. In 1932, became a Reichsleiter in the NSDAP and reorganized Nazi youth cells. Chief of the Social Office of the Reich Youth Leadership in 1933. Active service on Western Front until May 1940; August 1940, succeeded Baldur von Schirach as Reich Youth Leader. Severely wounded on Eastern Front, 1941, losing an arm. During the last weeks of the war commanded units of Hitlerjugend incorporated into the Volkssturm. Axmann was present in the Führerbunker; he escaped on 1 May 1945 together with Martin Bormann and Dr Ludwig Stumpfegger. Presumed dead, he lived for several months under the alias Erich Siewert; arrested December 1945, he was sentenced at Nuremberg in May 1949 to 39 months imprisonment.

Baur, Johann 'Hans' (1897–1993) Served in World War I with German air force. Became Adolf Hitler's pilot during 1920s–30s, and later his personal pilot. Stayed in the Führerbunker to the end; after Hitler's suicide tried to escape to the West but was captured by the Russians.

Below, Nicolaus von (1907–83) Entered the Reichswehr in 1929, transferred to Luftwaffe 1933; Hitler's Luftwaffe adjutant 1937–45. Escaped from Berlin on 30 April 1945; in British captivity until 1948.

Bormann, Albert (1902–89) Brother of Martin Bormann. Joined the NSDAP in 1924; from 1931 responsible for Hitler's Private Chancellery, from 1934 ADC to the Führer. In 1945 left Berlin for Obersalzberg, where he worked on a farm under a false name. Surrendered himself in 1949, but released that October.

Bormann, Martin (1900–45) In 1924, together with Rudolf Hess, accused of murder and imprisoned for one year. Joined NSDAP in 1927; chief-of-staff to Hess in July 1933. A Reichsleiter in October of that year, he was appointed head of the Party Chancellery on 29 May 1941, and rose to be Hitler's private secretary and the second most powerful man in the Reich. In 1945, took refuge in the Führerbunker together with his adjutant SS-Staf Wilhelm Zander and his secretary Else Krüger. After Hitler's death Bormann was named Party Minister in the new government. By 2 May he had left the bunker, supposedly with Stumpfegger and Axmann; died that day, perhaps by his own hand.

Brückner, Wilhelm (1884–1954) Studied law and economics; discharged as lieutenant in Bavarian infantry 1918, joined the Freikorp Epp. Joined NSDAP late 1922, and on 1 February 1923 became leader of the Munich SA Regiment. That November he took part in the Munich *putsch*; sentenced to 18 months' imprisonment but released four and a half months later. In 1930 became Hitler's adjutant and bodyguard, later rising to chief adjutant. In November 1934, Hitler appointed him SA-Obergruppenführer. He increasingly lost influence to Wehrmacht and SS adjutants after the outbreak of war, and on 18 October 1940 he was fired after an argument with Hitler's house manager Kannenberg, to be succeeded by Julius Schaub. He went into the Wehrmacht, becoming a colonel by May 1945.

Burgdorf, Wilhelm (1895–1945) Commanded 529th Infantry Regiment, May 1940–April 1942; became Deputy Chief of the Army Personnel

Wilhelm Brückner (right) in his office in the Chancellery. (© Ullstein: 00343642)

Department, promoted to Chief in October 1944. In that month he also became adjutant to Hitler; played a key role in the forced suicide of Field Marshal Rommel. He joined Hitler in the Führerbunker, and committed suicide on 1 or 2 May 1945.

Christian, Gerda, *née* Daranowski (1913–97) Began working as a secretary to Hitler in 1937; married Erich Kempka, divorced, and in February 1943 married naval officer Eckhard Christian. During a brief break from her employment she was replaced by Traudl Junge, but soon returned to Hitler's service. With a large group including fellow secretaries Else Krüger and Traudl Junge, tried to escape Berlin on 1 May but captured by Soviet troops on morning of 2 May.

Darges, Fritz (b.1913) Joined the SS on 1 April 1933, commissioned 12 September 1935. Joined NSDAP on 1 May 1937; from September 1936 to October 1939 adjutant to Reichsleiter Martin Bormann. In rank of SS-Sturmbannführer, became adjutant to Hitler on 1 March 1943. Pro-

moted SS-Obersturmbannführer in January 1944, he returned to active Waffen-SS service on 20 August. According to Martin Bormann, Darges was dismissed for being inattentive and too chatty with other staff members, and was transferred to the front at Hitler's order.

Dirr, Adolf, 'Adi' (b.1907) Blacksmith and semi-professional boxer, member of SA and NSDAP in 1929. Joined SS-Begleitkommando in 1932; sent to Obersalzberg on 22 April 1945. Taken prisoner May 1945, and released in 1948.

Dörnberg, Alexander Freiherr von (1901–83) Served after 1918 in para-military Freikorps. Studied law, then entered diplomatic service; posted to Washington DC, Bucharest, and London, where he became friendly with German ambassador Joachim von Ribbentrop. In 1934 Dörnberg joined the Party and in 1938 the SS; July 1938, head of protocol at Foreign Ministry. In this function he received British Prime Minister Neville Chamberlain, and accompanied Ribbentrop to Moscow.

Fegelein, Hermann Otto (1906–45) Former stable boy to Christian Weber, one of the wealthy original members of the Nazi Party. In 1928 joined Bavarian State Police; joined NSDAP and transferred to the SS in 1931; rose to command SS Main Riding School in Munich in 1937. In 1943, Fegelein briefly commanded SS Cavalry Div 'Florian Geyer' on Russian Front, and was injured. Attached to Hitler's staff as Himmler's adjutant and representative of the Waffen-SS, on 3 June 1944 he married Gretl Braun, sister of Eva. After Himmler tried to negotiate a surrender to the Allies in April 1945, Fegelein left the Führerbunker but was caught in his Berlin apartment wearing civilian clothes and in the company of a Hungarian mistress. After court-martial he was turned over to SS General Rattenhuber, and executed in the Chancellery garden on 29 April.

Flegel, Erna (1911–2006) Red Cross nurse who had worked alongside one of Hitler's physicians, Dr Werner Haase. From January 1943 transferred to Reichs Chancellery, where she served as a nurse for Hitler's entourage. She befriended Magda Goebbels and sometimes acted as a nanny to the Goebbels children.

Gesche, Bruno (b.1905) Member of the SS-Begleitkommando, and its commander from 15 June 1934 to 5 January 1945.

Grawitz, Professor Dr Ernst-Robert (1899–1945) 'Reichs Physician SS and Police'; advised Himmler on the use of gas-chambers, and carried out medical experiments on concentration camp prisoners. As a physician in the Führerbunker he petitioned to be allowed to leave Berlin; Hitler refused, humiliating him in front of several women. On 24 April, while eating with his wife and two children, he detonated from two hand grenades held beneath the table, killing them all.

Günsche, Otto (1917–2003) A Sturmbannführer in the Leibstandarte-SS, he became the Führer's personal adjutant, and was present at the 20 July 1944 bomb attempt. It was Günsche who burned the bodies of Hitler and Eva Braun in the Chancellery garden on 30 April 1945. A few hours later he left the bunker and was captured by Soviet troops; he was released in 1956.

Haase, Dr Werner (1900–50) Joined the Nazi Party in 1933 and the SS in 1941; served as Hitler's deputy personal physician 1935–45, rising to rank of SS-Obersturmbannführer. In late April 1945, together with Ernst Günther Schenck, he worked in the field hospital in the air raid shelter under the Reichs Chancellery. On 29 April he was summoned by Hitler to administer poison to his dog Blondi, so he could see whether the poison supplied by Dr Stumpfegger was effective. Haase remained in the bunker until Hitler's suicide and then returned to his work in the public shelter, where he was taken prisoner by the Soviets. Suffering from tuberculosis, he died in captivity.

Hentschel, Johannes (1908–82) Master electromechanic, hired for the Chancellery in July 1934. Responsible for the machine room in the Führerbunker, he was one of the last to leave, as he ensured that the underground field hospital had power. Released from Soviet captivity in April 1949.

Hewel, Walther (1904–45) One of the earliest members of the NSDAP, he took part in the Munich *putsch* and served time in Landsberg prison with Hitler, acting as his valet. After release he worked for several years as a coffee salesman and planter for a British firm; in Indonesia, he successfully organized local branches of the Nazi Party among German expatriates. During the 1930s Hewel returned to Germany and entered the diplomatic service. At the Foreign Ministry in March 1939 he transcribed the conference between Hitler and Czech president Emil Hácha. He later served as Ribbentrop's liaison to Hitler, and remained part of the Führer's inner circle. After escaping the bunker in the group led by Wilhelm Mohnke, he killed himself by biting a cyanide capsule while shooting himself in the head.

Hoffmann, Heinrich (1885–1957) Joined the NSDAP in 1920 and was chosen by Hitler as his official photographer. Hoffmann's photographs were published as postage stamps, postcards, posters and in books; both he and Hitler received royalties from all uses of Hitler's image, making Hoffmann wealthy. His daughter Henriette married the HJ leader Baldur von Schirach, and his second wife introduced his Munich studio assistant Eva Braun to Hitler. Hoffmann was sentenced to four years' imprisonment after the war.

Junge, Gertraud 'Traudl', née Humps (1920–2002)
Hired in November 1942 as a private secretary to
Hitler. In June 1943 she married SS officer Hans
Hermann Junge, who died in combat in 1944.
Typed Hitler's last private and political wills in the
bunker. Escaped on 1 May together with Baur,
Rattenhuber, Gerda Christian, Else Krüger, Constanze Manziarly and Dr Ernst-Günther Schenck
in the group led by SS-Brigadeführer Wilhelm
Mohnke. Captured on 2 May, she was repeatedly
raped by Soviet troops and was subsequently held
for a year as the 'personal prisoner' of a Russian
major before eventually returning to Germany.

Kannenberg, Artur 'Willi' (1896–1963) Former
cook, waiter and restaurateur; in 1930 he was
running a pub where Göring and Goebbels met.
In 1931 became mess manager at the Munich
Brown House, and in 1933 butler at the Reichs
Chancellery, from which he escaped in April 1945.

Kempka, Erich (1910–75) Worked as a mechanic
for the automotive manufacturer DKW; joined
the Nazi Party in April 1930, and was one of eight
founding members of the SS-Begleitkommando
in 1932. A reserve driver for Hitler's personal
entourage, in 1934 he replaced Julius Schreck and
Emil Maurice as Hitler's primary chauffeur, valet
and bodyguard, and ran the Chancellery motor
pool, garages and workshops. His wife Gerda (née
Daranowski) divorced him and married Eckard
Christian. On 30 April 1945 he was one of those
responsible for burning Hitler's corpse, leaving
the bunker the following day. On 20 June he was
captured by US troops at Berchtesgaden. At the
Nuremberg trials Kempka claimed to have seen
Martin Bormann killed by an anti-tank rocket
(see Appendix 4); he was released in October
1947.

Krebs, Hans (1898–1945) Volunteered for army
service in 1914, promoted lieutenant in 1915, and
remained in the Reichswehr after 1918, becoming
a general of infantry; served as military attaché in
Moscow shortly before the war. After service on
both Eastern and Western fronts he was
appointed Chief of the Army General Staff on 1
April 1945, which brought him to the
Führerbunker. On 1 May, Goebbels sent Krebs
and Colonel von Dufving out under a white flag
to deliver a letter suggesting surrender terms to

Soviet commanders – these were ignored. As the
Red Army closed in on the Führerbunker, Krebs
and General Burgdorf committed suicide.

Körber, August (b.1905) Member of the Party and
the SS from 1932; served from 1934 to 1945 in the
Leibstandarte-SS and the SS-Begleitkommando.
On 22 April 1945 he was ordered to take documents to the Obersalzberg, and fell into American
hands in May.

**Freytag von Loringhoven, Freiherr Bernd (1914–
2007)** Commanding a Panzer battalion in 1942,
he was flown out when his unit was encircled in
the Stalingrad pocket in January 1943. Rose to
general rank; from July 1944 until April 1945,
served as an adjutant to both General Heinz Guderian and General Hans Krebs as Army chiefs-of-
staff. In the bunker he was assigned the task of
preparing reports for Hitler; after 23 April these
were mainly based on whatever he could glean
from Allied sources such as Reuters and the BBC.
He left the Führerbunker during the evening of 29
April, accompanied by Gerhardt Boldt and Lieutenant-Colonel Rudolf Weiss, and spent two
years in British captivity. Freytag-Loringhoven
returned to the new Federal German Army (Bun-
deswehr) and was promoted general in 1956; he
was appointed Deputy General Inspector before
retiring in 1973.

Lehmann, Armin Dieter (b.1928) At the age of 16
he was drafted into the Volkssturm, and decorated with the Iron Cross. Selected by Artur
Axmann to be one of the 'Hitler Youth Heroes'
delegation to visit the Führer on his birthday, and
presented to Hitler in the Reichs Chancellery
garden outside the Führerbunker on 20 April
1945. Lehmann became one of Axmann's last
couriers, leaving the bunker shortly after Hitler's
suicide. He survived, and later emigrated to the
USA.

Linge, Heinz (1913–80) Hitler's valet, and one of
many officers, soldiers, servants and secretaries
who moved into the Reichs Chancellery bunker in
February 1945. There he continued as valet and
protocol officer, delivering messages to Hitler and
escorting people for whom Hitler had sent. One
of the last to leave the bunker, Linge was interrogated extensively by the Red Army. He was
released in 1955.

Hitler's personal valet, SS Lieutenant Heinz Linge. (Library of Congress)

Lorenz, Heinz (1913–85) Hitler's Chief Press Secretary during the war. In the Führerbunker he became part of a group who fabricated news by reviewing and re-writing Allied news reports, working for General Krebs and alongside General Freytag von Loringhoven and Gerhardt Boldt. It was Lorenz who, on 28 April, provided Hitler with confirmation that Heinrich Himmler was contacting the Allies through Count Folke Bernadotte.

Manziarly, Constanze (1920–45?) Began working for Hitler as a cook/dietician during his stays at the Berghoff in 1943. She left the Führerbunker on 1/2 May together with Gerda Christian and Traudl Junge in the group led by SS-Brigadeführer Mohnke, but disappeared shortly afterwards.

Misch, Rochus (b.1917) Orphaned at the age of two, he grew up with his grandparents and worked as a painter. In 1937 he joined the SS-Verfügungstruppe, the predecessor of the Waffen-SS, and was badly wounded in Poland, 1939. His

commanding officer recommended him for the Begleitkommando; thereafter, as a junior member of Hitler's permanent staff, he followed the Führer from headquarters to headquarters. In April 1945 he handled all direct communications from the Führerbunker. Captured by Soviet troops while attempting to escape on 2 May, he was released in 1954.

Mohnke, Wilhelm (1911–2001) Served as a company and battalion commander with 'Leibstandarte-SS Adolf Hitler' regiment in Poland, Low Countries, France and Balkans 1939–41, losing his right foot in Yugoslavia. Commanded a regiment of 12th SS Panzer Division 'Hitlerjugend' in Normandy and later commanded 1st SS Pz Div 'LSSAH' in the Ardennes. During the Battle of Berlin his Kampfgruppe Mohnke was charged with the defence of the Government District and Reichstag, independently of General Weidling's city-wide command. Under extreme pressure, Mohnke and his troops put up stubborn resistance in street fighting. After Hitler's suicide he planned to escape from Berlin towards the Western Allies on the Elbe. Mohnke left the Führerbunker on the evening of 1 May leading the first of three groups, but they were captured by Soviet troops the next morning while hiding in a cellar. Some of Mohnke's SS troops ignored General Weidling's order to surrender and maintained pockets of resistance until 8 May. Although he was wanted for ordering the murder of 80 British prisoners in May 1940 and 35 Canadians in July 1944, after surviving Soviet captivity 1945–55 Mohnke was allowed to live peacefully in West Germany until his death at the age of 90.

Morell, Theodor 'Theo' Gilbert (1886–1948) Studied medicine in Grenoble and Paris and obstetrics and gynaecology in Munich. Licensed in 1913, he served as a front-line medical officer during World War I. From 1919 he had a medical practice in Berlin, where he married Johanna Moller, a wealthy actress. In 1933 his society practice was threatened because many of his patients were Jewish; that April he joined the Nazi Party. In 1936 he treated Heinrich Hoffmann, Hitler's photographer, for gonorrhoea. Hoffmann and his assistant Eva Braun introduced Morell to the Führer. During a party at the Berghof he assured

Hitler, who was suffering from a skin rash and intestinal gas, that he could cure him within a year. When his treatment seemed to be effective Morell became part of Hitler's social inner circle; under his care, by April 1945 Hitler was taking 28 different pills a day along with numerous injections. On 22 April Hitler dismissed Morell from the Führerbunker, saying that he did not need any more medical help. Morell escaped Berlin on one of the last German flights, but was soon captured by the Americans. He was never charged with any crimes.

Naumann, Werner (1909–82) A State Secretary in Joseph Goebbels' Propaganda Ministry, he was appointed in Hitler's political testament to head it, since Goebbels was promoted to Reich Chancellor. Naumann left the bunker on 30 April 1945.

Puttkamer, Karl-Jesko von (1900–81) Entered the Imperial Navy as a cadet in 1917; became naval adjutant to Hitler in 1935. Promoted Korvettenkapitän in 1936, he took command of the destroyer *Hans Lody* in September 1938. Naval liaison officer at the Führerhauptquartier (Hitler's HQ) in August-September 1939, he then served as the Führer's naval adjutant until April 1945, being promoted vice-admiral on 1 September 1943. Injured by the 20 July 1944 bomb attempt.

Rattenhuber, Johann (1897–1957) Munich police officer, appointed head of Hitler's personal bodyguard in March 1933. Became an SS-Gruppenführer at the time of the 20 July bomb plot. In the Führerbunker on 30 April he was one of the group to whom Hitler announced that he intended to kill himself rather than be captured by the Soviets. On 1 May, Rattenhuber led one of the groups escaping from the bunker; captured that day, he was taken to Moscow. Sentenced to 25 years' imprisonment in February 1952, he was in fact released in 1955 and handed over to the German Democratic Republic, who allowed him to go to West Germany.

Schädle, Franz (b.1906–45?) Civil engineering technician who joined the NSDAP and SS in 1930. In 1933 he entered the Leibstandarte-SS and the SS-Begleitkommando, of which he took command on 5 January 1945. Wounded, he was unable to leave the Chancellery and was taken

prisoner; some sources say he shot himself on 1 May 1945.

Schaub, Julius (1898–1967) SS officer, with the final rank from 1944 of SS-Obergruppenführer. Hitler's adjutant 1922–40, chief adjutant 1940–45. Ordered by Hitler in April 1945 to fly out of Berlin and burn all papers and personal belongings in his homes in Munich and the Obersalzberg.

Schroeder, Emilie Christine 'Christa' (1908–84) Worked as a stenographer in Munich for the SA high command, and for Hitler from shortly after his appointment as Reich Chancellor in 1933 until his death.

Stumpfegger, Dr Ludwig (1910–45?) Member of medical teams at 1936 Summer Olympics in Berlin and Winter Olympics in Garmisch-Partenkirchen. His sanatorium was used by the SS in 1939, and he participated in medical experiments on women inmates of Ravensbrück concentration camp. In 1945 he worked directly for Hitler in the Führerbunker under the direction of Dr Morell. At Hitler's request, he administered a cyanide tablet to the Führer's German Shepherd dog 'Blondi', to see how quickly it worked; it is said that he helped Magda Goebbels murder her children. After 9pm on 1 May he left the Führerbunker in a group that included Martin Bormann and Artur Axmann, and probably died on 2 May.

Voss, Hans-Erich (1897–1969) Graduated from the Imperial Naval Academy in 1917, and served in the Kriegsmarine throughout the Weimar Republic and Third Reich. Commander of the heavy cruiser *Prinz Eugen* in 1942, he met Goebbels when the minister toured the ship. Impressed by Voss, Goebbels arranged to have him appointed naval liaison officer to Hitler's headquarters in March 1943. Wounded during the bomb attempt on Hitler on 20 July 1944. On 30 April 1945 Admiral Voss was among the group of officers who were informed that Hitler had decided to commit suicide. On 1 May, Voss joined the group led by SS-Brigadeführer Mohnke which tried to escape from Berlin; captured by the Soviets, he was brought back to the bunker for questioning, and to identify the bodies of Joseph and Magda Goebbels and their six children. He was sentenced to 25 years' imprisonment, but released to the German Democratic Republic in December 1954.

Weidling, Helmuth Otto Ludwig (1891–1955) A soldier since 1911, he fought in Poland, 1939, as colonel of the 56th Artillery Regiment; in France, 1940, and in the early stages of Operation 'Barbarossa', as artillery commander of XL Panzer Korps. He was promoted general of artillery in 1944, and in April 1945, as commander of a Panzer Corps, began his involvement in the Battle of Berlin. He was appointed by Hitler as commandant of the Berlin Defence Area on 23 April, and was ordered to defend the city to the last man. From about 26 April he was based at the old army headquarters in Bendlerstraße, since it had well-equipped air raid shelters and was close to the Reichs Chancellery. By nightfall on the 27th, Weidling's forces were completely cut off from the rest of Germany, and on the evening of 29 April the fighting line was only yards from his HQ in the Bendlerblock. Weidling discussed with his divisional commanders the possibility of breaking out to the south to link up with Wenck's 12th Army, whose spearhead units had reached Ferch on the banks of the Schwielowsee near Potsdam. The breakout was planned to start at 10pm on 30 April; when Weidling reached the Führerbunker that day he learned that Hitler had committed suicide. When the first attempt to secure a ceasefire failed, Weidling sent his chief-of-staff Colonel Theodor von Dufving to arrange a meeting with General Chuikov; this ended at 8.23am on 2 May 1945, and later that day loudspeakers announced Weidling's surrender to the remaining defenders. The Soviet forces flew Weidling to the Soviet Union where, on 27 February 1952, a military tribunal sentenced him to 25 years' imprisonment for not surrendering Berlin sooner. He died in captivity on 17 November 1955.

Wolf, Johanna (1900–85) Party member, who joined Hitler's personal secretariat in 1929 as a typist and became a senior secretary in his Private Chancellery in January 1933. On 22 April 1945, Hitler sent Wolf and Christa Schroeder to his house at Berchtesgaden in Bavaria, instructed to burn all personal papers. Wolf was taken prisoner by the Americans on 23 May in Bad Tölz, and remained in captivity until January 1948. Unlike Traudl Junge, she always refused to give interviews or to write her memoirs.

Appendix 4

Testimony from the *Führerbunker:* Erich Kempka

On 20 June 1945, Hitler's senior driver Erich Kempka, captured at Berchtesgaden, was interrogated by the US authorities regarding the last days of Hitler's life. His testimony was taken seriously, since he was considered to be 'not a very clever man'; the American intelligence officers did not believe Kempka had the ability to simply invent a story like this. In these extracts from the transcript a few trivial changes have been made to spelling, grammar and syntax to make it clearer for modern British readers.

The airport cars

. . . On 20 April 1945 I went for about one-quarter of an hour to the Führer's bunker in order to congratulate the Führer upon his birthday. There was no special ceremony in the Führer's bunker.

On the evening of 20 April 1945 I got the order to prepare about 12 vehicles by means of which persons belonging to the Führer's headquarters and [some of] their relatives were taken to the Berlin airfields [at] Staaken, Tempelhof, Schönwalde and Gatow. These were about 80 persons, among them Rear-Admiral von Puttkamer, SS-Sturmbannführer Goehler [representative of SS-Gruppenführer Fegelein], Miss Schroeder and Miss Wolf. On 21 April a number of vehicles were prepared in which 40 to 50 persons were driven to several airfields. Cars for a direct drive from Berlin to Munich were not despatched by me before or after this date. During the night of 22/23 April the personal physician of the Führer, Prof Dr Morell, two stenographers, the consulate sec-

retary Doehler and several women were driven to the airfield at Gatow.

Though I did not get any definite statement from authorized sources, I supposed that the Führer would remain in Berlin after 22 April. During the days before 20 April I often heard [the Führer say] that he would remain in Berlin [whatever happened]. In the days after 20 April I repeatedly asked SS-Sturmbannführer Günsche whether I was to secure the vehicles, because they were [being] gradually destroyed by artillery fire. SS-Sturmbannführer Günsche told me that . . . the Führer at any rate would stay at the Reichs Chancellery. . . . The buildings of the Reichs Chancellery were repeatedly set on fire in the days after 22 April. The fires were extinguished only very primitively.

Himmler's treachery

Communications to the outside were cut after about 25 April. In those days a story was distributed by the German press bureau that Himmler had turned to the Western powers and had stated that the Führer was suffering from a cerebral haemorrhage, was completely ill and would not live for much longer. I had not read this story myself, which was said to have been printed in the newspapers. As far as I am aware Himmler did not appear in the Reichs Chancellery during the days around 20 April or later.[90]

Persons present in the bunker

. . . As far as I recollect Foreign Minister von Ribbentrop did not see the Führer, at any rate not after 20 April. After 22 April the following still stayed with the Führer: General Krebs, General Burgdorf, Vice-Admiral Voss, Reichsleiter Martin Bormann, Reichsminister Dr Goebbels with his wife, Dr Naumann (Secretary of State in the Propaganda Ministry), SS-Hauptsturmführer Schwegermann as adjutant of Dr Goebbels, SS-Gruppenführer Fegelein, SS-Sturmbannführer Günsche, SS-Sturmbannführer Linge, SS-Gruppenführer Rattenhuber and SS-Standartenführer Dr Stumpfegger. I personally saw Reichsleiter Bormann several times up to the morning of 2 May 1945. . . . The children of Reichsminister Dr Goebbels, who were brought to the bunker of the Reichs Chancellery on 22 April, were taken away with a nurse only on 1 May [sic]. . . . According to what I have seen and heard Field Marshal Keitel and Colonel-General Jodl must have left Berlin already on 22 April.

The execution of Fegelein

SS-Gruppenführer Fegelein telephoned me, I believe on the afternoon of 28 April, and asked me to come and see him in the Führerbunker that evening in order to receive important papers concerning the Führer, the Reichsführer-SS and himself personally, in order to destroy or to hide them so well that they could not be found in case the Russians should get through to the Reichs Chancellery. I went to the Führerbunker towards evening in order to meet SS-Guppenführer Fegelein, [but] I did not meet him. Reichsleiter Bormann asked me where Fegelein was; I [told him] that SS-Gruppenführer Fegelein had ordered a car and had driven to his home. They endeavoured to find [him]; later I heard that SS-Gruppenführer Fegelein had reappeared at the Reichs Chancellery in civilian clothes and had been interrogated there by an SS-Gruppenführer Müller, whom I had never seen before and who was said to belong to the SS-Hauptamt or to the SD.[91] Fegelein is said to have admitted to Müller that he had several times been at Nauen in order

to meet the Reichsführer-SS there; he had endeavoured to get out of the Reichs Chancellery [and to] get through to the Reichsführer-SS in civilian clothes. According to what I was told Fegelein was declared guilty of high treason and shot by order of SS-Gruppenführer Müller.

The wedding

In the days after 20 April 1945 I still saw Hitler several times in his bunker . . . He had not changed in his behaviour and gave a quiet impression. Eva Braun stayed with the Führer. After 28 April there were rumours in the Reichs Chancellery that the Führer and Eva Braun had been married during the night of 28/29 April. [An official] of the Propaganda Ministry had performed the ceremony. At the same time two orderlies had been married. There was no announcement of the marriage of the Führer to Eva Braun, [and] I did not congratulate the Führer. Only on 1 May did Secretary of State Dr Naumann confirm the marriage of the Führer.

I spoke to the Führer for the last time on 29 April. I reported to him that I was engaged in bringing food into the central part of Berlin . . . in order to supply the hospitals in the Government District. In the Reichs Chancellery itself there was a field hospital. The Hotel Adlon, the [regional headquarters] of the NSDAP of Berlin, and other buildings had been converted into hospitals. The bunkers of the Reichs Chancellery, where several hundreds of wounded had been quartered, had not suffered any damage from artillery fire. There was no enemy infantry attack on the Reichs Chancellery until the morning of 2 May.

The petrol cans

On 30 April at 2.30pm SS-Sturmbannführer Günsche telephoned me to come to the Führerbunker. I was also to ensure that five cans of gasoline, that is to say 200 litres, were brought along. I at once took along two or three men carrying cans. More men were following, because it took some time to collect 200 litres of gasoline. By order of SS-Sturmbannführer Günsche the cans were brought by these men to the entrance of the

Führerbunker located in the garden of the [Old] Reichs Chancellery, which was next to the so-called 'tower-house' and about 20 metres from the side of the so-called Haus Kempka, my quarters. After depositing the cans the men at once returned [to the garage]. There was an SD sentry at the entrance of the bunker. I then went into the antechamber of the briefing room, where I met SS-Sturmbannführer Günsche. Günsche told me that the Führer was dead. He did not tell me any details . . . he just explained he had been ordered by the Führer to burn him immediately after his death, 'so that he would not be exhibited at a Russian freak-show'.

A short time after that SS-Sturmbannführer Linge and an orderly whom I do not remember came from the private room of the Führer carrying a corpse wrapped in an ordinary field-grey blanket. Based on the previous information from SS-Obersturmbannführer Günsche I at once supposed that it was the corpse of the Führer. I could only see the long black trousers and the black shoes, which the Führer usually wore with his field-grey uniform jacket. Under these circumstances there was no doubt that it was the corpse of the Führer. I could not observe any spots of blood on the body wrapped in the blanket. Thereupon Reichsleiter Martin Bormann came from the Führer's living room, carrying in his arms the corpse of Mrs Eva Hitler, née Braun. He turned the corpse over to me. Mrs Hitler wore a dark dress. I did not have the feeling that the corpse was still warm. I could not recognize any injuries on the body. The dress was slightly damp only in the region of the heart.

Behind Reichsleiter Bormann there came also Reichsminister Dr Goebbels. SS-Sturmbannführer Linge and the orderly now went upstairs with the corpse of the Führer to the bunker exit towards the garden of the Reichs Chancellery; I followed with the corpse of Mrs Hitler. Behind me came Reichsleiter Bormann, Dr Goebbels and SS-Sturmbannführer Günsche. Reichsleiter Bormann wore uniform. According to my recollection Dr Goebbels also wore uniform. It [must have been] shortly before 3pm, as I remember that I received the first warning from Günsche at 2.30pm and needed five or ten minutes to reach

the Führerbunker. Linge and the orderly carried the corpse of the Führer from the westward bunker exit in the tower-house and put the wrapped corpse on the flat ground in a small depression, which was about 4 to 5 metres distant from the bunker exit. There was no lawn, just bare sand; in the last period construction work was being done in the Reichs Chancellery. I put the corpse of Mrs Hitler next to the Führer's. Immediately SS-Sturmbannführer Günsche poured the complete contents of the five cans over the two corpses and ignited the fuel.

Reichsleiter Martin Bormann, Reichsminister Dr Goebbels, SS-Sturmbannführer Günsche, SS-Sturmbannführer Linge, the orderly and I stood in the bunker entrance, looked towards the fire and all saluted with raised hands. Our stay in the bunker exit lasted only a short time because the garden of the Reichs Chancellery was under heavy artillery fire; [the brief period outside] the bunker exit already posed a danger to our lives. The ground of the garden of the Reichs Chancellery was ploughed by shellholes. Besides us, the event could only have been observed by the tower-post sentry of the SD; however, he was not notified of what had happened.

Upon returning into the Führerbunker no words were exchanged. Günsche, Linge and another person went into the living room of the Führer. In order to return to the garage I had to pass through the Führerbunker and wanted to look once more at the rooms in which the Führer had lived his last days. I followed the persons mentioned into the living room . . . Opposite the entrance of the room . . . stood a narrow sofa. In front of the right front leg of the sofa lay a Walther pistol, 6.35mm calibre, which I knew belonged to Miss Eva Braun. Also on the floor approximately in front of the middle of the sofa lay a Walther pistol, 7.65mm calibre, that I supposed belonged to the Führer. I myself did not touch anything in the room, but stood there silently for a few seconds only. I did not ask any questions and no one else spoke to me. According to the situation it was clear to me that the Führer and Miss Eva Braun had shot themselves. From the location of the two pistols I concluded that the Führer sat about on the middle of the sofa before firing the shot and that Eva Braun had sat on the right part of the sofa . . .

The attempted escapes

. . . In the late afternoon of 1 May 1945 I received official notice from SS-Sturmbannführer Günsche, who was the commandant of the Reichs Chancellery, that on the same evening at 9pm the break-out from the Chancellery was to take place. All men who were able to walk and wanted to go along, as well as the women who had belonged to the Führer's staff, were to take part. SS-Brigadeführer Mohnke was designated as the leader of the group to break out . . . The persons included in the break-out party assembled at 9pm in the coal-bunker of the new Reichs Chancellery . . . [they] may have amounted to 500 or 700, among them a number of women. All available weapons – rifles, sub-machineguns, pistols, automatic carbines, light machine guns and Panzerfausts – were distributed to Groups 1 to 6. SS-Brigadeführer Mohnke took the lead and led Group 1 [including] Ambassador Hewel, SS-Sturmbannführer Günsche, Mrs Christian, Mrs Junge, and Miss Krüger – about 50 to 60 persons.[92]

The men and women left the Chancellery singly through a narrow hole in the wall along Wilhelmstraße, near the corner of Wilhelmstraße and Voss-Straße. Because of the heavy artillery fire everyone ran as quickly as possible to the next entrance of the subway. The nearest entrance, of the Kaiserhof stop about 50 metres from the Reichs Chancellery, had collapsed after a direct artillery hit. Therefore we went to the entrance approximately 200m distant . . . [here Kempka has gone forward in time to describe his own party's later escape] which was located opposite the Hotel Kaiserhof. This entrance was open. At the subway [U-Bahn] station the single groups gathered again and went to the Friedrichstraße station along the subway tracks. There were many civilians on the platforms of the subway station [and] soldiers sat around on the stairs. As leader of my group, which consisted of approximately 60 drivers, I left the subway station through one of the exits which are located north of the city railway [S-Bahn] station in the Friedrichstraße.

Outside everything was quiet. Without danger I went . . . up to the roadblock on the Weidendammer Bridge.[93] A few metres beyond the roadblock I came upon a group of soldiers who told me that shortly before a group of 50 to 60 persons had passed this spot towards the north. This was the leading Mohnke group. The soldiers declared that they had already tried to break through, but that they had been beaten back. Russian troops had occupied the houses and basements on both sides of the Friedrichstraße north of the Weidendammer Bridge. I then returned and fetched my men from the subway station [so that they could] take cover in the Admiralspalast which was located in front of the subway exit. After several groups had arrived . . . another break-through [attempt] was decided upon.

I made one . . . attempt with my group. We [got] through the second roadblock on the Weidendammer Bridge without being fired upon. But 10 or 20 metres beyond the second roadblock we received strong machine-gun fire from all sides, and had to retreat again. Further break-out attempts were [made], which failed. The break-through of the first group probably succeeded only because of the surprise of our opponents. Later on I met Mrs Junge on a march. She told me that the leading group under SS-Brigadeführer Mohnke had had to [stop] after a few hundred metres. About 5.30am [on 2 May] a negotiator appeared and made known that General [Chuikov] wished a temporary armistice until 6.15am. During these negotiations Mrs Junge together with the other women had left the basement. Ambassador Hewel had taken poison. SS-Gruppenführer Rattenhuber, who also belonged to Group 1, had received a serious injury.

Martin Bormann

During our stay in the Admiralspalast, Reichsleiter Martin Bormann, State Secretary Dr Naumann, Schwegermann (the adjutant of Dr Goebbels), and other senior personalities appeared at about 2am or 3am. I [told] Reichsleiter Bormann that it was impossible to push through without heavy weapons. Later on, five or six tanks and armoured [reconnaissance] cars arrived which were manned by soldiers. It was decided that the tanks were to attempt the breakthrough and that the men who had broken out of the Reichs Chancellery were to advance under the protection of the tanks. Behind one tank State Secretary Dr Naumann went as the first in the top of the tank turret [sic ?], behind him [went] Reichsleiter Martin Bormann followed by SS-Standartenführer Dr Stumpfegger. I went behind Dr Stumpfegger. More men joined us.

After the tank had gone about 30 to 40 metres it received a direct hit with a Panzerfaust [German anti-tank rocket – Kempka presumably used the term generically for any such weapon]. The tank flew apart. I saw a short flash of lightning and [fell] to the ground where I remained lying unconscious. My last impression was that Dr Naumann, Bormann and Dr Stumpfegger fell together and remained lying. I could [not see any specific] injuries. Because Dr Stumpfegger who preceded me was 30cm taller than I, he protected me from the full blast and I escaped with splinter injuries to my thigh and upper arm. After an undetermined period I regained consciousness, saw only fire around me, and crept back on the ground. I got behind the roadblock and sat down on the street because just then I could not see clearly. SS-Standartenführer Beetz was the first whom I saw.[94] He had a serious head injury. Just then I saw a new attack started from our side, but I decided not to go along any more because of its futility. I returned to the Admiralspalast, assembled my men and told them that they were dismissed. Each one could go on his own, to join a combat group or go home. I also advised them to procure for themselves civilian clothes.

I myself returned to the Friedrichstraße railway station with seven men, among them the lieutenant of the armoured troop, Joerke, who had been assigned to us with three armoured halftracks. We crossed the Spree River on the footbridge directly under the city railroad. We were able to reach a house on the northern bank of the Spree without being fired upon, and from there . . . up to a spot in the region of Albrechtstraße, Karlstraße or Ziegelstraße. The city railway runs along there. We reached a [yard] of the city railroad in which a dump of medical equipment was located. There we met two Yugoslavs and two Russian civilians [forced labourers]. . . They at once sympathized with us and promised to procure civilian clothes for us. When some of us had already got civilian clothes the first Russian soldiers arrived at the yard. We hid Lieutenant Joerke, who [was still in uniform, and] the others quickly changed their clothes. . . .

Evasion and capture

. . . The Russian soldiers procured food and drinks. I participated [in this celebration], which lasted until 2 o'clock of the following night [?]. After[wards] the Yugoslav woman left, but returned in the morning and brought me a coat. In this disguise I was able to leave the house and walked via Tegel to Henningsdorf. In Henningsdorf I was stopped by Russian soldiers and brought into a yard. There were German soldiers who all wore civilian clothes. We spent a few hours there. We were asked for papers. Nine-tenths of the men had no papers. Nevertheless all of us were dismissed.

(Kempka then gave an understandably rambling account of his attempts to reach the Elbe; in the course of several days he was repeatedly stopped, arrested, searched and eventually dismissed by various Soviet troops, during which adventures he was both accused at gunpoint of being a 'Werewolf', but also handed back his wallet and given a cigarette.[95] He swam what he thought was the Elbe on the night of 13/14 May, but it turned out to be only a tributary, and he was captured and held in a camp at Havelberg for 16 days. Released once more, he finally got across the Elbe to Gottberg and Vorsfelde in the British zone, where he was given a movement permit to Salzburg.)

Recollections

I still remember the following details. On the morning of 2 May, SS-Hauptsturmführer Schwegermann notified me that Dr Goebbels and his wife . . . had both died in the Führer's bunker . . . I did not ask any further questions, but I suppose that Dr Goebbels and his wife had committed suicide.

General Burgdorf and SS-Sturmbannführer Schädle of the Führer Escort Command still remained in the Reichs Chancellery. Schädle told me that he would shoot himself if the Russians were to get through to the Reichs Chancellery. So far as I know no other members of the Führer Escort Command remained there. It is possible that some returned after futile break-through attempts.

After 20 April, Reichsminister Speer came to the Reichs Chancellery in a [Fieseler Fi 156] Stork which was flown by Thea Rasche. I expect that the plane had landed on the Hofjägerallee.[96] However, the Führer at once sent Speer away. I do not believe that aircraft had landed and [taken off] on the East-West axis [, where] soon after 22 April heavy artillery fire was falling . . .

Following an interrogation on 30 June of Hermann Karnau, a member of the SD who had seen the corpses of Hitler and Eva Braun, Kempka made a supplementary statement on 4 July.[97] He substantially stuck to his account:

To the statement of Karnau that at 4pm on 1 May he saw Hitler still alive, and that at 6.30pm he witnessed the cremation of the two bodies, I cannot agree. I remember clearly that I was called by SS-Sturmbannführer Günsche on 30 April by telephone to come over and have some gasoline brought there. From that I conclude that the cremation happened around 3pm. It is possible that Karnau witnessed other cremations. During those days [on many occasions] two, three, four or five cans of gasoline were asked for . . . important papers were burned in the vicinity of the bunker exit.

I agree with a great part of the story Hermann Karnau gave about the cremation, but with a small part I do not agree. I don't know Herman Karnau personally . . . I only knew some of the members of the SD Police at the Führer Headquarters. Karnau could have been the guard who was at the exit of the Führer's bunker leading into the garden . . . This guard [must have been] present there at the cremation. Because of the heavy artillery fire, he could not have been in the garden of the Reichs Chancellery, but he had to be by the entrance of the bunker. He must have been standing close to the rest of them during the cremation.

I think it is impossible that Karnau recognized the Führer by his moustache shortly before the cremation; the upper part of Hitler's body was fully covered by a blanket. I don't think it possible that, by laying the body on the ground, the blanket was blown back sufficiently to uncover the head . . . All that could be seen were the feet, which stuck out 15 to 20 centimetres. The black low-cut shoes, black socks, black trousers which the Führer usually wore could be seen.

Eva Braun, as I said before, was easy to recognize. She was not covered by a blanket. She wore shoes with high heels, and it is possible that [they] had cork soles. . . . Contrary to Karnau's statement, I remember that Eva Braun was also laid on her back so that her face was upwards. I still remember that because of the wind her skirt was blown up so that her garters could be seen. The place where both were lain out was about 3 or 4 metres away from the exit of the bunker. Hitler and Eva Braun were not lying parallel to each other, but Eva Braun's body was at an angle to Hitler's. Hitler's body was on the left, and Eva Braun's body was on the right, as seen from the exit of the bunker . . .

Karnau's statement that Dr Stumpfegger was present at the cremation . . . could be true. I said in my statement of 20 June that SS-Sturmbannführer Linge and an 'orderly' carried Hitler's body. Now I believe that it is possible that the person I called an orderly could have been Dr Stumpfegger, since it was Dr Stumpfegger who pronounced Hitler and Eva Braun dead. . . .

Later, when he was interviewed in 1974 by James O'Donell for his book *The Bunker*, Erich Kempka said: 'In 1945, to save my own skin, I told American and British interrogators what they wanted to hear'. Hitler's chauffeur was not unique in this; later in life, even Albert Speer had a reputation for 'You pay what I want, I say what you want'.

Bibliography

Anon, *Hitler's Neue Reichskanzlei, 'Haus des Grossdeutschen Reiches, 1938–1945; Zeitgeschichte in Farben'* (Arndt-Verlag, Kiel, 2002)

Anon, *After the Battle No.61: The Reichs Chancellery and the Berlin Bunker Then and Now* (Battle of Britain International Ltd, Old Harlow, UK, 1988)

Below, Nicolaus von, *At Hitler's Side, The Memoirs of Hitler's Luftwaffe Adjutant 1937–1945* (Greenhill Books, London, 2004)

Dietmar, Arnold, *Neue Reichskanzlei und "Führerbunker"* (Ch. Links Verlag, Berlin, 2005)

Eberle, Henrik & Uhl, Mattias, *The Hitler Book, The Secret Dossier Prepared for Stalin* (John Murray, London, 2005)

Groehler, Olaf, *Dag Tagebuch Europas – 1945, Die Neue Reichskanzlei – Das Ende* (Brandenburgisches Verlaghaus, 1995)

Groehler, Olaf, *Illustrierte Historische Hefte, Das Ende der Reichkanzlei* (VEB Deutscher Verlag des Wissenschaften, Berlin, 1976)

Hitler, Adolf, *Die Reichskanzlei, in Kunst im Dritten (Deutschen) Reich* (1939)

Hoffmann, Peter, *Hitler's Personal Security: Protecting the Führer, 1921–1945* (Da Capo Press, USA, 2000)

Lotz, Wilhelm, 'Der Neubau der Reichskanzlei', in *Kunst dem Volk* (1/1939)

Lotz, Wilhelm, 'Die Errichtung der Neuen Reichskanzlei' in *Die Neue Reichskanzlei* (Munich, 1940)

Lotz, Wilhelm, 'Die Innenräume der Neuen Reichskanzlei' in *Die Neue Reichskanzlei* (Munich, 1940)

Mabire, Jean, *Mourir à Berlin – Les Français, derniers défenseurs du bunker d'Adolf Hitler* (Jacques Grancher, Paris, 1995)

Misch, Rochus, *J'étais garde du corps d'Hitler* (Le Livre de Poche, Paris, 2007)

Peeters, Michel, *Beelden voor de Massa, Kunst als wapen in het Derde Rijk* (Houtekiet, Antwerpen, 2007)

Schönberger, Angela, *Die Neue Reichskanzlei von Albert Speer* (Gebr Mann Verlag, Berlin, 1981)

Schramm, Percy E., *Kriegstagebuch des Oberkommandos der Wehrmacht, 1940–1945*, 8 Vols (Bernard & Graefe Verlag, Munchen, 1982)

Spotts, Frederic, *Hitler and the Power of Aesthetics* (Hutchinson, London, 2002)

Notes

Chapter 1: Wilhelmstraße No.77

(1) Otto Eduard Leopold von Bismarck, Count of Bismarck-Schönhausen, Duke of Lauenberg, Prince of Bismarck (1815–98) – the leading Prussian and German statesman of the 19th century, and immensely influential in European affairs. As Minister-President of Prussia 1862–90 he organized the unification of Germany under Prussian leadership, and upon the formal creation of the German Empire – the First Reich – in Jan 1871 he served as its first Chancellor.

(2) The von der Schulenburgs were a Brandenburg, later Prussian noble family which originated in 1237 with Ritter Wernerus de Sculenburch. Its male members provided the Prussian Army with a number of marshals, generals and other senior officers over the generations; others were ministers, diplomats and bishops. Two Schulenburgs – Fritz Dietlof, and Friedrich Werner, Graf von der Schulenburg – took part in the assassination plot against Hitler which culminated in the failed bomb attempt of 20 July 1944; both were hanged.

(3) The Radziwill family were descended from Lithuanian *boyars* who had advanced their fortunes considerably during the 15th century; eventually it split into five branches, and members acquired and retained great wealth and influence in Poland, Lithuania and Belarus during the 500 years before 1939.

(4) Prince Leopold (etc) von Hohenzollern (1835–1905) was head of the Swabian branch of his family. After the Spanish revolution that overthrew Queen Isabella II he was offered the crown of Spain by the new government. The offer was (ostensibly) supported by Bismarck, but (predictably) opposed by the French Emperor Napoleon III. Leopold was forced to decline the offer, but it had served the purpose of goading France into a war that she could not win.

(5) Bismarck's creative report of this private conversation between King Wilhelm and the ambassador was carefully worded, and leaked, to create the false impression that the king had insulted the ambassador. French public and media opinion was volatile, and crowds were soon marching through Paris chanting 'To Berlin!'. Napoleon was aware that his army was quite unready for war, but by then he was the prisoner of events.

(6) Field Marshal Helmuth Karl Bernhard, Graf von Moltke (1800–1891), for 30 years chief-of-staff of the Prussian Army – one of the great strategists of the latter 19th century, organizer of a modern method of directing armies in the field, and victor of the Franco-Prussian War of 1870–71. He is usually referred to as Moltke the Elder, to distinguish him from his nephew Helmuth, chief-of-staff of the German Army on the outbreak of World War I.

(7) The Congress of Berlin (13 June-13 July 1878) was a conference of the major European powers and the Ottoman Empire to discuss the vexed affairs of the Balkans. It solved nothing, and resulted in intensified differences between Russia and Austria-Hungary – which served Germany's purposes.

(8) Prince Maximilian (etc) of Baden (1867–1929) was noted as a liberal. Appointed Chancellor of Germany in Oct 1918 in order to negotiate an Armistice with the Allies, he formed a government including the socialists Friedrich Ebert and Philipp Scheidemann. With Germany in a revolutionary situation, he announced the Kaiser's abdica-

tion without the latter's consent, and resigned in favour of Ebert on 9 Nov 1918; the proclamation of the German Republic followed immediately.

(9) Friedrich Ebert (1871–1925), leader of the moderate wing of the Social Democratic Party (SPD). For several months during the German revolution of 1918–19 he led an entirely socialist government as chancellor; when a Constituent Assembly met at Weimar in Feb 1919, Ebert was chosen as first President of the German Republic.

(10) Philipp Scheidemann (1865–1939), SPD politician who proclaimed the Republic on 9 Nov 1918, and served from Feb 1919 as first chancellor of the Weimar Republic under Ebert's presidency. He resigned in June 1919 during disputes over the Treaty of Versailles.

(11) Wilhelmstraße No.73, the former Kaiser-lichen Haus- und Hofministeriums, served as the German Presidential Residence after World War I.

(12) Although the title 'chancellor' was not used between 11 Nov 1918 and the first session of the Constituent Assembly in Feb 1919. German chancellors between 13 Feb 1919 and 28 Jan 1933 were:
Philipp Scheidemann (13 Feb–20 June 1919)
Gustav Bauer (21 June 1919–26 Mar 1920)
Hermann Müller (27 Mar–8 June 1920)
Konstantin Fehrenbach (25 June 1920–4 May 1921)
Joseph Wirth (10 May 1921–14 Nov 1922)
Wilhelm Cuno (22 Nov 1922–12 Aug 1923)
Gustav Stresemann (13 Aug–30 Nov 1923)
Wilhelm Marx (30 Nov 1923–15 Jan 1925)
Hans Luther (15 Jan 1925–12 May 1926)
Wilhelm Marx (17 May 1926–12 June 1928)
Hermann Müller (28 June 1928–27 Mar 1930)
Heinrich Brüning (30 Mar 1930–30 May 1932)
Franz von Papen (1 June–17 Nov 1932)
Kurt von Schleicher (2 Dec 1932–28 Jan 1933).

(13) Built for the businessman and manufacturer Albert Borsig (1829–78), son of the indus-trialist and locomotive engineer August Borsig. Albert never actually moved into it, and died a year after its completion.

(14) Paul (etc) von Beneckendorff und von Hin-denburg (1847–1934) had retired from the Prussian Army in 1911, but was recalled at the outbreak of World War I. He became a national hero after the victory of Tannen-berg on the Eastern Front in 1914, and in 1917 became commander-in-chief. He and his chief-of-staff Erich Ludendorff rose to eclipse the Kaiser himself in public esteem, and Hindenburg retained this respect – justly enough, it was Ludendorff who was blamed for the catastrophes of summer-autumn 1918. Retiring again in 1919, Hindenburg was elected second President of Germany in 1925. At the age of 84, he was obliged to run for re-election in 1932 as the only candidate who might defeat Adolf Hitler; he did so in a run-off. In Jan 1933 he was obliged to appoint Hitler as chancellor, and thereafter was easily manipulated.

(15) Prof Dr Ing Eduard Jobst Siedler (1880–1949); after the extension project he also worked in 1938–39 on the Reichs-luftschutzschule (anti-aircraft school) at Heckeshorn am Wannsee. Robert Paul Kisch also worked for the German Army on the Seeckt-Kaserne barracks in Berlin Spandau, the Reiter-Kaserne in Fürsten-walde and the Cavalry School in Potsdam Krampnitz.

(16) Wilhelm Marx (1863–1946), a Roman Catholic senior jurist who was President of the Senate of the Reichskammergerichte in Berlin under the Weimar Republic, and served two terms as chancellor.

(17) How the architects felt about this typically political cant is unrecorded. The modern reader is irresistibly tempted to respond, 'No pressure, then. . .'.

Chapter 2: Hitler in the Wilhelmstraße

(18) Dr Heinrich Brüning (1885–1970)

(19) Franz (etc) von Papen zu Köningen (1879–1969), a Roman Catholic nobleman, soldier, diplomat and politician. Although he played

a central role in Hitler's appointment as chancellor, he was acquitted when indicted during the post-war Nuremberg trials, since the tribunal decided that his 'political immoralities' fell outside its jurisdiction.

(20) General Kurt von Schleicher (1882–1934), the last Chancellor of Germany before Hitler, would be murdered by the SS during the purge of 30 June 1934, 'the Night of the Long Knives' – see note 37 below.

(21) Alfred Hugenberg (1865–1951), a right-wing businessman, press proprietor and member of the Reichstag. Briefly a member of Hitler's first cabinet, he was forced to resign in June 1933 and to sell his media companies to the Nazis, but retained his parliamentary seat until 1945.

(22) The flat consisted of 10 rooms totalling 463 square metres (4,983 square feet).

(23) KPD – *Kommunistische Partei Deutschlands,* German Communist Party.

(24) DNVP – *Deutschnationale Volkspartei,* German National People's Party.

(25) SPD – *Sozialdemokratische Partei Deutschlands,* German Social Democratic Party.

(26) Paul Ludwig Troost (1878–1934), designer and architect. Before World War I he had designed steamship decor; his work for such transatlantic liners as the *Europa* demonstrated a combination of Spartan traditionalism with modernity.

(27) The Brown House in Munich, named for the colour of the Party and SA uniforms, was the national headquarters of the NSDAP, opened in Jan 1931. It was severely damaged by Allied bombing in Oct 1943 and was largely destroyed by the end of the war; what remained was cleared in 1947.

(28) Dietrich Eckart (1868–1923), one of the first important members of the NSDAP and a participant in the 1923 Munich 'beerhall *putsch*'.

(29) Heinrich Tessenow (1876–1950), architect and urban planner active in the Weimar era.

(30) Karl August Hanke (1903–1945), NSDAP official who served as Gauleiter of Lower Silesia 1940–45. On 29 Apr 1945 he was appointed in Hitler's will to replace Himmler

as Reichsführer-SS; he was subsequently shot while attempting to escape from a prisoner-of-war camp at Neudorf.

(31) *The Führer's Buildings.*

(32) Inspector General of Construction for the State Capital (i.e. Berlin).

(33) Hans Heinrich Lammers (1879–1962), a lawyer, and after World War I a member of the Stahlhelm veterans' association. He joined the NSDAP in 1932, looked after the Party's legal affairs, and was invited to join Hitler's first cabinet in Feb 1933 as a State Secretary. He later rose to be a Minister and Chief of the Reich Chancellery staff, providing a reliable link between the Führer and his government. Lammers played a central role in the drafting of such legislation as the Nuremberg race laws and the euthanasia programme. Lammers' wife and daughter committed suicide on 8 and 10 May 1945; he was tried at Nuremberg in 1949 and sentenced to 20 years' imprisonment, but was released in 1954.

(34) Ernst Julius Röhm (1887–1934) was a Bavarian officer veteran of World War I and of the post-war Freikorps anti-Communist militia. Still a serving officer in the Reichswehr, he joined the NSDAP in 1920 and was prominent in the organization and arming (with Army weapons) of the Sturmabteilungen. Like Hitler, he was imprisoned following the abortive *putsch* of Nov 1923. Angered by Hitler's insistence on avoiding in future any appearance of a 'private army' in rivalry with the Reichswehr, Röhm left Germany in 1928 to take up a military advisor's post in Bolivia. In 1930 Hitler invited him back to head the SA.

(35) The Reichswehr was officially established on 1 Jan 1921, in accordance with severe limits on its size and level of equipment imposed under the Treaty of Versailles: 100,000 men, without tanks, heavy artillery or aircraft. While never friends to social democracy, under such capable commanders as Gen Hans von Seekt the Reichswehr remained obedient to the governments of the Weimar Republic. After Hitler became Reich Chan-

cellor of Germany on 30 Jan 1933 the forces were encouraged to begin a secret programme of expansion and re-equipment; the Versailles limits were formally abandoned with the public proclamation of conscription for the new Wehrmacht, revealed in March 1935.

(36) On 11 Apr 1934, Hitler negotiated with military leaders aboard the warship *Deutschland;* to gain their support he was willing to pay their price of suppressing the SA and guaranteeing the rights of the Reichswehr as the only armed force in the country.

General Werner von Blomberg (1878–1946) was Minister of Defence in Hitler's 1933 cabinet. He was appointed professional commander-in-chief of the armed forces in 1935, and in 1936 was the first field marshal created by Hitler. Von Blomberg was forced to resign all his posts on 27 Jan 1938 following a scandalous marriage to a young former prostitute, and spent World War II in obscurity.

(37) The SS had originally been a constituent part of the SA, being formed in Apr 1925 as Hitler's personal bodyguard. In June 1934 it had three battalions of armed gendarmerie; thereafter the organization would grow at enormous speed, becoming the main enforcement arm of the Party's will. Himmler would quickly take over the leadership of the whole state police and security apparatus, but SS control was not limited to these obvious functions. Through a combination of intimidation, reward and overlapping membership, over a few years the SS would greedily infiltrate every state organization, and gather to itself power (and wealth) in every sphere of national life, forming a sort of parallel state-within-the-state whose actual role became indefinable.

The premier armed unit, the Leibstandarte-SS Adolf Hitler ('Adolf Hitler Life Regiment'), formed in September 1933, would provide the ceremonial guard battalion for the Chancellery. By the outbreak of war six years later the military arm of the SS – the SS-Verfügungstruppe, later retitled

Waffen-SS – was ready for combat in modest numbers, fighting in Poland and the West. At first Himmler's ambitions for his organization to contribute a branch to the Wehrmacht were largely ignored by both Hitler and the Wehrmacht; but after two of its fledgeling divisions distinguished themselves in Russia in winter 1941–42, the Waffen-SS was steadily expanded and became a favoured recipient of the most motivated men and the best equipment. By 1944 it was the only branch of the armed forces that Hitler really trusted.

(38) The control of the budget for this contract was so strict that, for example, Speer wrote to Lammers explaining that workers had not been paid for the half-hour they spent listening to Hitler's radio speech during Hindenburg's funeral.

(39) The significance of this oath – binding all members of the armed forces to unquestioning obedience not to the German State or its constitution, but to the person of Adolf Hitler – was obviously a major factor in the later behaviour of the senior command of the Wehrmacht.

(40) Prof Leonhard Gall had worked for Paul Troost, and had helped to complete the House of German Art after the latter's death.

(41) The balcony was reinforced with 8mm steel plate to protect Hitler and his entourage against assassination attempts.

(42) Letter from Albert Speer to Dr Lammers, 16 May 1933.

(43) Aktion T4 would continue, even after the alleged 'euthanasia halt' of August 1941. While it became the concern of a separate unit, away from the Führer's Chancellery, that department remained responsible for about 100 employees of the extermination clinics who were transferred to the extermination camps of *Aktion Reinhardt,* even after they came under the command of Odilo Globocnik.

Bouhler and his wife committed suicide on 19 May 1945 after being apprehended by US troops, and while they were being transported to an imprisonment facility at the former Dachau concentration camp.

(44) WRV, Weimarer Verfassung. This was the constitution that governed the Weimar Republic 1919–33; technically, it remained in effect throughout the existence of the Third Reich until May 1945.

(45) Rudolf Hess (1896–1987) made an unauthorized and still unexplained flight to England in May 1941, and spent the rest of the war in captivity. He was tried and convicted at Nuremberg, and spent the rest of his life in Spandau Prison in fragile mental health.

Martin Bormann (1900–45), Chief of the Party Office from May 1941 and Hitler's personal secretary from Oct 1943, was the second most powerful man in Germany in the latter half of the war, and far more energetically active than his Führer. He was long rumoured to have escaped from Berlin in May 1945, but his death during the attempt is now confirmed.

Chapter 3: *Die Neue Reichskanzlei*

(46) In 1935 the Ebertstraße was renamed Hermann-Göring-Straße.

(47) During 1922, Julius Lippert (1895–1956) participated in the assassination of Foreign Minister Walther von Rathenau, and joined the NSDAP. Appointed State Commissioner for Berlin in 1933, he was responsible for much of the early persecution of Jews in the capital. After a dispute with Albert Speer, Lippert was dismissed in 1940; Hitler wrote of him that he was 'an incompetent, an idiot, a failure, a zero'.

(48) After the war, Piepenberg and another former supervisor on the New Chancellery building site, Otto Appel, proposed that Speer work for them. Both died in 1966 while Speer was still in prison.

(49) It is a German tradition that everyone involved in a construction project celebrates the completion of the roof on a new building by a *Richtfest* or 'topping-out' ceremony. The architect, contractor or owner of the building makes a traditional speech com-

mending the workers and asking for the grace of God; he then hammers the last nail into the roof, empties a glass of schnapps, and throws the glass over the edge. If it shatters when it hits the ground, all will be well – otherwise it is a bad omen, and a blot on the reputation of the contractor. Proceedings continue with the adornment of the *Richtbaum* – a sort of maypole – and a long and well-lubricated feast or *Richtschmaus*.

Chapter 4: Description – the Exterior

(50) Statues by the Viennese sculptor Ambrosi were planned for the four corners of the pool, but these were never realized.

Chapter 5: Description – the State Apartments

(51) Hermann Kaspar (1904–86). A pupil of Edmund Steppes, he distinguished himself at the Munich Academy of Arts and became a protegé of Bestelmeyer, the president of the Academy, to whom he owed his first significant commission – the mosaic freize for the Congress Hall at the Munich German Museum. In 1938 he was commissioned by Speer to create mosaics, floors and intarsia for the New Chancellery, and in the same year was appointed to a professorship at the Munich Academy. As a member of the cultural elite of the Third Reich he was dismissed in 1945, but later reinstated. He subsequently received many commissions, and taught several pupils who would themselves become famous.

(52) Kurt Schmid-Ehmen (1901–1968) studied sculpture 1918–21 under Prof Adolf Lehnert at the Academy for Graphic Art and Stone-Sculpture in Leipzig. After working as an apprentice stonemason, he studied under Prof Bernhard Bleeker at the Academy of Fine Arts in Munich, 1925–31. His work began to be internationally known and exhibited in 1935, and in 1937 he won the Grand Prix at the World Exposition in Paris. His creativity as a sculptor continued to flower right up until his death in 1968.

(53) According to Speer, Hitler particularly relished the central panel of Mars, depicting a sword half-drawn from the scabbard: 'Good, good . . . When the diplomats sitting in front of my desk see this, they will learn the meaning of dread.'

(54) See Chapter 7, Works of Art in the Chancellery.

Chapter 6: The Adminsitrative Quarters, and Hitler's Private Apartments

(55) Known as the Congress Hall, where Chancellor von Bismarck presided over the Congress of Berlin in June-July 1878.

(56) Heinz Linge, Karl Krause and Hans Junge.

Chapter 7: Works of Art in the Chancellery

(57) Later, all the employees of the Lobmeyr company were granted the status of *Kriegswichtig* – 'important to the war effort' – and were thus spared from military conscription. As a result the entire staff, and the company, survived the war.

(58) Hermann Gradl (1883–1964).

(59) Maria Anna Angelika (aka Angelica Katharina) Kauffmann (1741–1807), a Swiss-Austrian painter.

(60) Werner Piener was one of the contemporary German artists who became prominent by reason of his artistic achievements and his ground-breaking role (he made a major contribution to the revival of the art of tapestry). He was influential as a teacher, and as the director of the Hermann Göring School sponsored by the Reichsmarschall. His works, both landscape and symbolic, were commissioned for a number of major public buildings.

(61) They have been lost without trace since the end of World War II.

Chapter 8: 'How Adolf Hitler's Command Post Functions'

(62) See also Ch 2, under 'The State Secretary of the Reich Chancellery'. Although there were in theory 17 ministries, the normal system of cabinet government – with a first minister presiding over meetings of ministers each responsible for and representing the views of a department of state – no longer existed. There simply was no formal machinery for co-ordinating the work of ministries, and smaller, centralized bodies answerable directly to Hitler were superimposed above the level of Reich Minister. The most important was the Ministerial Council for the Defence of the State, established on 30 Aug 1939, comprising Göring (Chairman), Hess (Deputy Führer), Frick (Administration), Funk (Economy), Lammers (Head of Reich Chancellery) and Gen Keitel (Joint Services Chief-of-Staff).

Additionally, what Nunn calls in this article 'Special Services' were given powers arching across the nominal responsibilities of several Reich Ministers – Commissioners-General, Inspectors-General, Commissioners and Inspectors for Administration, Economic Affairs, War Production, the Four-Year Plan, and so forth. This article mentions in passing Dr Schacht – the economist Hjalmar Schacht, Minister for Economic Affairs, Aug 1934–Nov 1937; President of the Reichsbank until 1939, and Minister without Portfolio until 1944. (Arrested by the Gestapo for suspected contacts with the German internal resistance, he escaped trial.) Schacht was acquitted by the Allies at Nuremberg – his supposed powers as a Reich Minister had been largely imaginary.

If readers object that all this must have caused immense problems of demarcation, they are right: the 'management' of the highest echelons of the Third Reich was an abysmally inefficient tangle of rival empires. This situation was deliberately created by Hitler: determined to rule by his individual will alone, he exercised it not on institutions but on other individuals, letting them fight for his favour.

Chapter 9: History: the Chancellery at War

(63) Monsignor Josef Tizo (1887–1947) was a Roman Catholic priest who became a deputy of the Slovak People's Party in the Czechoslovakian parliament, a member of the Czechoslovakian government, and finally, from 1939–45, President of the Slovak Republic – a puppet state of Nazi Germany. He was hanged by the Czechoslovakian authorities after the war.

(64) The 'Blood Order' was officially known as the Decoration of 9 Nov 1923. Originally exclusive to participants in the Munich *putsch* of that date, this prestigious medal was later extended – to the putschists' dismay – to anyone who had served time in prison for Nazi activities, or who had been severely injured in the service of the Party, before 30 Jan 1933. Its last recipient was Reinhard Heydrich, who received it posthumously in 1942. The solid silver medal bore on the reverse a depiction of the Feldherrnhalle in Munich, a swastika, and the inscription UND IHR HABT DOCH GESEIGT ('And You Were Victorious After All'). Its recipients wore a ribbon of scarlet edged with black and white arranged in a unique fan-shape around the button on the right breast pocket of uniforms.

(65) At that time the Reichstag functioned in the Kroll Opera House.

(66) The U-Bahn is the Berlin underground railway system.

(67) *Showa* was the Japanese term for the reign of the Emperor Hirohito.

(68) Gian Galeazzo Ciano, Count of Cortellazzo and Buccari (1903–44), Italian Minister of Foreign Affairs 1936–43, was Mussolini's son-in-law. This did not prevent him playing an active part in the conspiracy that deposed *Il Duce* in Sept 1943, when Italy changed sides; nor – after he had been captured by the Germans – did it save him from a firing squad ordered by his father-in-law.

(69) The reporter got a couple of details wrong: Hans Valentin Hube (1890–1944) was decorated on 20 Apr not with the Oakleaves but with the supreme grade of the Knight's Cross, the Diamonds. Known as 'Clever Hans', Hube was an extremely courageous and able officer, who had lost an arm in 1914 but returned to the Western Front in a combat command. In 1943–44 he distinguished himself as a corps and later an army commander in Sicily, Italy and the southern USSR.

(70) The major Red Army offensive that smashed Germany's Army Group Centre and cleared Belarus and eastern Poland of German troops between 22 June and 19 Aug 1944.

(71) Roland Freisler (1893–44) was a prominent and notorious Nazi judge, who became State Secretary of Hitler's Reichs Ministry of Justice, and President of the Volksgerichtshof (People's Court). Established without constitutional authority, this apparatus tried those deemed hostile to Hitler's regime for a wide variety of newly created offences, often defined in deliberately vague terms. Freisler was most infamous for his conduct of a series of show-trials, such as those of the members of the 20 July 1944 bomb plot.

(72) Hermann Giesler (1898–1987) studied architecture in the late 1920s at the Academy of Applied Arts in Munich, and set up as an independent architect in 1930. He was commissioned to build Hitler's house in Munich, and in 1938 was appointed to the General Building Inspectorate for the redevelopment of the city of Munich. In 1941 he was entrusted with the planning for a wholesale redevelopment of the city of Linz; he started working on the plans and a large-scale model in 1942.

Chapter 10: Hitler's Last Headquarters

(73) Julius Schaub, Hitler's chief adjutant from 1940, memorably compared the shelters to 'a U-boat prowling the depths below Berlin's sea of houses and ministry buildings'.

(74) After Hitler opened this facility to Berlin's hospital and welfare services, many an infant 'Adolf' first saw the light here; births were marked by flowers for the mother and a

bankbook with a 100RM deposit for the child. During Apr 1945 it was converted to a field hospital, and shelters for a battalion of the Leibstandarte-SS and for Bormann's staff; the maternity clinic was moved to a shelter beneath the Reichstag building.

(75) Hitler's dog-handler, SS Sgt Tornow, also served in the Bunker.

(76) Hitler's presence in Berlin was only revealed three months later, in a radio broadcast by Goebbels on 22 Apr 1945.

(77) Wilhelm Mohnke (1911–2001) – see Appendix 3. He formed his battle-group from the remnants of nine SS units, including the Guard Bn 'LSSAH', the Training & Replacement Bn 'LSSAH' from Spreenhagen, the Führer-Begleit-Kompanie and the Reichsführer-SS Begleit-Bataillon.

(78) On 6 Mar 1945, north of Lake Balaton in Hungary, the elite 6th SS Panzer Army commanded by SS Gen 'Sepp' Dietrich – one of Hitler's oldest and most loyal followers – had taken part in a counter-offensive codenamed Operation 'Spring Awakening'. This had ground to a halt by 14 Mar, due both to deep mud and strong Red Army resistance. Hitler's fantasies took no account of the massive attrition suffered by even his most favoured formations, such as the 1st SS Pz Div 'Leibstandarte-SS Adolf Hitler' that spearheaded the advance. He reacted to its inevitable failure with rage, and ordered SS Gen Dietrich to have his men strip the treasured *'Adolf Hitler'* cuff-bands from their tunics. Dietrich, disgusted, did not bother to relay this insult to his troops.

(79) The Führer Intelligence Detachment was supposed to prevent information leaving the Führerhauptquartier.

(80) Some sources date his departure as 21 April.

(81) Herrgesell stated when interviewed that he and his colleague Haagen were flown out to the Obersalzberg on the evening of 22 Apr; in fact they both left on the 24th, when the last few planes (except for Hanna Reitsch's) left Gatow airfield.

(82) The S-Bahn was a rapid transit rail system, partially over- and partially underground.

(83) A runway was laid out on the East-West Axis between the Brandenburg Gate and the Victory Column.

(84) Gen Weidling's forces consisted of surviving elements of the following formations, though by now these were *ad hoc* battlegroups mostly of limited size and capability: 9th Luftwaffe Paratrooper Div (Col Hermann) at Lichtenburg; SS Armoured Infantry Div 'Muncheberg' (SS Gen Mummert) at Karlshorst; 20th Armd Inf Div (Gen Scholze) at Zehlenhof; 18th Armd Inf Div (Gen Rauch) at Tempelhof; 11th SS Volunteer Armd Inf Div 'Nordland' (SS Gen Ziegler, from 25 Apr SS Gen Krukenberg) at Oberschöneweide, incorporating c.300 French SS volunteers of the former SS Assault Brigade 'Charlemagne'. Personnel from the Luftwaffe 1st Flak Div (Gen Sydow) mainly manned the Berlin anti-aircraft towers.

One source places survivors of 23rd SS Vol Armd Inf Div 'Nederland' (SS Gen Wagner) in central Berlin; others have them almost wiped out at Fürstenwalde east of Berlin, the survivors surrendering to US troops at Magdeburg early in May.

(85) Mohnke's headquarters was situated in the Chancellery air raid shelter, with two satellite HQs in shelters under the Air Ministry (LtCol Seifert) and State Opera House (SS Gen Krukenberg).

(86) Hitler's Luftwaffe adjutant, Col Nicolaus von Below, refused to sign the personal will.

(87) Ferdinand Schörner (1892–1973), a determined general and Nazi loyalist, was promoted field marshal on 4 Apr 1945 – the last German ever to achieve that rank. Commanding Army Group Centre on the Eastern Front, he abandoned his troops and flew west to surrender to US forces on 11 May 1945. Hitler's will appointed him commander-in-chief of the German Army (OKH). After the war he was imprisoned by both the USSR and West Germany.

(88) SS Col Zander – described by his British interrogator Maj Hugh Trevor-Roper (later

the historian Lord Dacre) as a 'half-educated, stupid but honest man' – had tried to refuse the mission, and in the event simply hid the documents on a farm where he found employment. They were later recovered by Trevor-Roper's colleague Weiss – Hitler's personal will, the political testament, and the marriage certificate of Adolf Hitler and Eva Braun.

(89) See testimony in Appendix 4.

Appendix 4

(90) Remark by the reporter: Himmler wanted to see the Führer on 22 Apr, but Hitler refused; he did not wish to be swayed by anybody from his decision to remain in Berlin.

(91) SS Gen Heinrich Müller – 'Gestapo' Müller – had been the head of the Secret State Police since 1935. It is entirely in character that Kempka should never have seen him; he was the most determinedly secretive of all the Nazi leadership, and was hardly ever photographed. He was last seen in the Bunker on 29 Apr; no trace or hint of his fate after that day has ever been found.

(92) Else Krüger was Bormann's secretary, and spent the battle of Berlin in the Führerbunker. She left on 1 May with the group led by SS Gen Mohnke, which was captured in a cellar the following morning by Soviet troops. Note that when Kempka speaks of 'Mrs Christian' he is referring to his own ex-wife – see Appendix 3.

(93) About 300m north of the Friedrichstraße railway station.

(94) SS Col Beetz was Hitler's second command pilot, subordinate to SS Gen Baur.

(95) 'Werewolf' was the codename for clandestine resistance groups that were supposed to carry out guerrilla attacks against the occupying forces at the end of the war. They were almost completely inactive and ineffective.

(96) This is confusing, as there seem to have been two German pioneer women pilots flying Fieseler Fi 156 Storks into the Government District in the same week. Thea Rasche (1899–1971) is recorded as Germany's first (licensed ?) woman pilot. However, more famously, Hitler's appointee to succeed Göring in command of the Luftwaffe, Gen Robert Ritter von Greim, was flown into Berlin in a Stork on 26 Apr, by the more celebrated Hanna Reitsch (1912–1979). Appointed as a Luftwaffe test-pilot in 1937 by Gen Udet, Reitsch successfully test-flew many types including the lethal Me 163 rocket-plane and the piloted test version of the V1 flying bomb. She flew out of Gatow by night on 27/28 or 28/29 Apr in an Arado Ar 96. Reitsch continued to fly competitively, and four months before her death aged 67 she achieved a new woman's world long-distance gliding record of 500 miles (805km).

The Hofjägerallee was a transverse road crossing the East-West Axis highway.

(97) After the war Karnau declared: 'I was commanded by an SS officer to leave my post . . . The entrance to the Führer's bunker was locked. I went back and tried to get in by the emergency exit, the one leading to the Chancellery garden. As I reached the corner between the tall sentry-post and the Führerbunker proper . . . I suddenly saw what looked like a petrol-rag being thrown. In front of me lay Adolf Hitler on his back and Eva Braun on her stomach. I definitely established that it was him . . . Half an hour later I returned to the spot. I could no longer recognize him because he was pretty charred. I spoke to Erich Mansfeld, who was on sentry duty in the tower, and he also confirmed "There lies Adolf Hitler – he is burning." I left this place . . . and by the staircase I met SS-Stubaf Schädle, who confirmed that the Chief was burning . . . in the Chancellery garden. At about 6pm I returned . . . Hitler and Eva Braun had now burned to the point that the skeletal structure could clearly be seen. Whether during the period from 6pm to 8pm petrol was again poured over the remains I don't know, but when I was there again at 8pm ashes were already drifting in the wind. . .'.

Index